LBSCR
ATLANTICS

LBSCR ATLANTICS

JEREMY ENGLISH

Ian Allan
PUBLISHING

First published 2014

ISBN 978 0 7110 3791 5

Published by Ian Allan Publishing Ltd, Hersham, Surrey, KT12 4RG.

Printed in Bulgaria

Visit the Ian Allan Publishing website at www.ianallanpublishing.com

FRONT COVER TOP LEFT The second Brighton Atlantic, H1 No 38, seems to have been somewhat camera-shy and this is the first of only two photographs in this book of it in working order. Thus it has star billing at the top of our cover! Madgwick Collection

FRONT COVER TOP RIGHT The sad story of the smaller Marsh Atlantic tanks is a significant theme throughout this book. This photograph of I2 No 15 at Epsom Downs station on 3rd June 1909 was possibly the high point of their careers. It had just headed the Royal Train with their Majesties King Edward VII and Queen Alexandra aboard. Hopefully (there's no actual record of this) it didn't stall on the way as had its I1 sibling a year previously! Madgwick Collection

FRONT COVER MAIN IMAGE Seemingly freshly outshopped but in fact condemned, the 'Last British Atlantic' rests in the yard at Eastleigh after working its final train, on 24 April 1958, to the heart of the LBSCR's erstwhile rival. Just one of its nameplates would be officially preserved, being presented to the town of Eastbourne, close to the famous chalk headland after which the locomotive was named. Colour-Rail BRS359

BACK COVER No 40, destined to be the shortest-lived of the H1 Atlantics, is seen in its prime heading an untypical Brighton 'fast' service consisting of a 'Pullman Pup' luggage-and-generator van, two Pullman carriages, two LBSCR 'Balloon' coaches and a very old non-corridor carriage at the back. It seems the further back in the train you rode, the lower you were in the strict class system of the Edwardian Age. Madgwick Collection

PAGE 1 No 32424 *Beachy Head*, the last working express passenger Atlantic locomotive on British Railways, is seen in its final condition at the very end of its working life, at Newhaven on 13 April 1958, having just arrived from Victoria with the 'Sussex Coast Express' railtour, a commemorative run organised by the Railway Correspondence & Travel Society. Colour-Rail 394348

PREVIOUS PAGE No 39 in charge of a Pullman train in snowy conditions near Stoat's Nest. Madgwick Collection

CONTENTS

INTRODUCTION

The Brighton Atlantics are something of an enigma inasmuch as they were not designed for the railway on which they ran, were completely outside the normal locomotive policy of that railway yet were to prove to be the longest-lived and final working examples of all the Atlantic-type locomotives used in Great Britain. (Incidentally, the name 'Atlantic' derived from US practice whereby the first railroad to use a particular locomotive type would lend its name to that type, the Atlantic Coast Railroad having been the first *successful* user of 4-4-2s, in 1894; there had been a few experimental but poorly designed examples built from 1888 which were soon scrapped).

This book might almost have been entitled *The Accidental Atlantics*, for its principal subjects were built as the result of an urgent need by the London, Brighton & South Coast Railway (usually referred to as the LBSCR or simply 'the Brighton') for powerful express passenger locomotives after the company's Locomotive, Carriage & Wagon Superintendent, Robert John Billinton, had died in office in late 1904 without having produced a truly modern express passenger locomotive design. The early years of the 20th century were a time of enormous change in steam-locomotive technology.

The LBSCR's directors appointed Douglas Earle Marsh to succeed Billinton. Marsh was the Chief Assistant Mechanical Engineer of the Great Northern Railway, at Doncaster Works, where his immediate superior, Henry Ivatt, had introduced the first British Atlantic class in the form of his Class C1 express passenger tender engines for that company in 1898.

The urgency of the situation led Marsh, shortly after his appointment by the Brighton, to borrow a set of 'C1' drawings from Ivatt and to have five very similar machines built for his new employer, these being the celebrated Class H1 tender engines. Soon after that he produced a series of four types of Atlantic tank engines and, nominally at the end of his time at Brighton, a final series of six tender engines.

This book tells the story of these six classes. None survived the 1950s, but they had made their mark, so much so that a re-creation of an example of the final design was to be built in the early

ABOVE No 2421 *South Foreland*, the first of the final class of Brighton Atlantics, in the form in which they became most famous, as modified by Maunsell but in Bulleid's green livery. It is seen outside Newhaven shed, which provided motive power for the Cross-Channel boat trains to London (Victoria) – services which were the prime responsibility of these most handsome locomotives at the time this photograph was taken during the summer of 1947. Colour-Rail SR47

years of the 21st century on the famous Bluebell Railway in Sussex, a former Brighton secondary line which saw the Brighton Atlantics in their working days. As a result, present and future generations of railway enthusiasts and travellers will be able to appreciate for themselves the elegance and sheer presence of one of the most beautiful of all British steam-locomotive designs.

Jeremy English

Sherfield English, Hampshire

June 2014

CHAPTER 1

GENESIS – NOTHING TO DO WITH THE BRIGHTON

ABOVE The first British Atlantics were the 22 Ivatt Class C1 (later LNER Class C2) locomotives of the Great Northern Railway. Here No 949, the first production example, built in 1900, is seen on 30 July 1921 at Potters Bar. Madgwick Collection

It may seem perverse to start the story of the 'Brighton Atlantics' with a chapter declaring itself to be 'nothing to do with the Brighton', but that, essentially, sums up the genesis of what would become the 'Brighton Atlantics', so please bear with me as I describe how they came about.

At the start of the 20th century the railways of Great Britain were in the midst of a major transition. The network of lines was virtually complete, and attention was turning to the improvement of services as passengers increasingly patronised those companies which offered 'modern' facilities such as dining cars with corridors and gangways as well as toilets for all; they also demanded faster schedules. These facilities were available – at a cost, in the form of premium fares – in the privately owned Pullman trains, most notably on the Brighton, which both ran complete Pullman trains and inserted Pullman cars into others. However, these demands all came at another cost – additional weight. 'Catch 22' applied: additional weight needed more power, as did increased speeds, so more powerful engines were needed; the traditional 4-4-0 types which had dominated British passenger work since the 1880s were rapidly becoming outclassed. (It is assumed herein that readers are familiar with the Whyte system of describing locomotive types by the numbers of driven and carrying wheels.)

Fortunately, during the final decade of the 19th century there had been a generational change amongst the Chief Mechanical Engineers of many British railway companies, and the best of the new men were keen to innovate, the changing demands giving them the full scope they needed. Nowhere was this more evident – nor contrasting – than in the locomotive departments of the railway companies which served the country's east and west coasts. Britain's longest main-line railways ran northwards into Scotland, rivalry between the companies serving Scotland being exceptionally fierce, the two principal routes being known as the West Coast and East Coast main lines.

The West Coast was served by the largest British railway company of all, the London & North Western Railway (LNWR), which broadly covered the principal industrial areas on the western side of England, having an end-on connection at Carlisle with the

Caledonian Railway serving Scotland. The LNWR main line and the Caledonian main line formed the West Coast main line. The LNWR's locomotive policy had long been dominated by the fanatical Francis Webb, who from the 1880s onwards had foisted upon it some quite extraordinary types of locomotive and left the company in 1903 with something of a motive-power problem. Its partial recovery under George Whale would become intertwined with the story of the Marsh Atlantics.

The Midland Railway passed through the middle. A latecomer to the Anglo-Scottish traffic competition, it had a CME, Samuel Johnson, who pursued a 'small engine' locomotive policy which under his successor (from 1903) Richard Deeley would stagnate for the rest of the company's existence and cause a crisis in London, Midland & Scottish Railway (LMS) days, once the Midland and LNWR had amalgamated.

Development of higher-powered locomotives for the West Coast main line generally involved the 4-6-0 type, although none would prove particularly successful. Fortunately, the genesis of the Marsh Atlantics lay on the East Coast.

The East Coast main line from London to Edinburgh had been built up piecemeal by three large railway companies, the Great Northern (GNR), North Eastern (NER) and North British (NBR), and they had to keep up with or exceed the developments on the West Coast. To the first of these companies goes the credit for introducing the Atlantic (4-4-2) type to Great Britain, thanks to the appointment in the mid-1890s of one of the more adventurous of the new generation of CMEs.

The advantage a trailing axle gave to the steam-locomotive designer lay in the deep firebox that could be provided behind the trailing coupled wheels; the early designs of 4-4-0 and, more particularly, 4-6-0 were constrained by the difficulties inherent in providing a large enough grate above the driving axles. Another constraint was the grade of steel then available; some engineers thinking that additional coupled wheels would restrict locomotive speeds, owing to the difficulties of ensuring all the wheels were of exactly the same diameter, combined with the increased frictional resistance of all the additional machinery. Some had even

reverted to the use of single driven wheels, most notably Samuel Johnson on the Midland – and Patrick Stirling on the GNR.

Perhaps because it directly served fewer heavily industrialised towns and cities than did the West Coast line, the East Coast line had attached a greater importance to its express passenger trains and would remain at the forefront of the search for speed in the steam era, culminating in the enduring world speed record for steam set in 1938 by the great *Mallard*. This achievement had its roots in Patrick Stirling's magnificent 8ft Singles, high-stepping locomotives which sped the lightweight trains of the mid-Victorian era northwards. To many these represented the peak of British steam-locomotive elegance; Stirling considered the appearance of a locomotive every bit as important as its efficiency, and the Singles stood out as being almost perfect in both respects. Although rapidly becoming outclassed, these highly successful machines were still in charge of expresses between London and York in 1895, when Stirling, aged 75, died in office on 11 November and Henry Alfred Ivatt, at the age of 44, succeeded him as Chief Mechanical Engineer of the GNR. This would bring about what was perhaps the greatest sea-change in locomotive policy that had occurred on any British railway up to that time.

The Singles being 4-2-2s, the logical way of improving the design of express locomotives was to add a further driving axle to create a 4-4-2, and this is what Ivatt, together with his newly appointed Chief Assistant CME and Manager of Doncaster Works, Douglas Earle Marsh, did, omitting the 4-4-0 stage (although they did introduce 4-4-0s for secondary work). Both men took office at the beginning of 1896, and it was thus an entirely new team that set about modernising the Great Northern's locomotive fleet. The first British Atlantic emerged from Doncaster Works at the end of May 1898. In some ways it echoed the principles that Stirling had espoused, being an extremely elegant design; one particular feature that emphasised this approach was that the boiler had a 1ft 11in extension ring which made the smokebox appear that much shorter than it actually was, thereby preserving the symmetry of the design. The 'long boiler' effect was also in the tradition of the East

Coast companies, albeit that of the North Eastern Railway, harking back to the days of Robert Stephenson.

The first locomotive, No 990 *Henry Oakley*, was officially experimental. It acquired the nickname 'Klondyke' (or 'Klondike') after the American Yukon Gold Rush of 1896, and the association may well have been arisen because this was the first British design to adopt the American practice of naming a locomotive type according to its wheel arrangement. It appeared just two months before the almost-as-famous Lancashire & Yorkshire Railway 'Highflyer' Atlantics designed by John Aspinall, but the latter displayed none of the beauty of design sported by the 'Klondykes', the successful experiment of No 990 resulting in a class total of 21 machines (plus one experimental four-cylinder example) by 1903.

Before the final batch of 'Klondykes' was delivered in 1903 a single enlarged version

was built. No 251 used the same basic running gear of the design (even having the same cylinders and motion) but a much larger boiler. Ivatt is reported as having been impressed with an oft-repeated saying of Stirling's predecessor on the GNR, Archibald Sturrock, that 'the measure of the power of a [steam] locomotive is its capacity to boil water'. In theory No 251 had that to an extent seldom seen before on British designs, for its principal feature was a wide firebox extending almost the entire width of the locomotive, this being made possible by the small carrying wheels on the trailing axle of the Atlantic's 4-4-2 wheel arrangement. This would become a feature on most British Pacific (4-6-2) designs, the ultimate express passenger steam locomotives on the country's railways – and the logical extension of the Atlantic layout.

It has often been asserted that the introduction of the wide firebox was at the instigation of the Chief Assistant CME, Marsh. He had had experience of the GWR's final types of broad-gauge locomotive, which had the wide fireboxes that the 7ft 0¼in gauge permitted. The short, wide grate was easier to maintain and fire than was a long narrow one, and this was seen as a major advantage. However, No 251, in service from 31 December 1902, and 20 production locomotives introduced in May and June 1904 were not immediately successful. The width of the firebox meant that it was not possible to fit the normal screw reversing gear, and a lever gear was used instead. This was difficult to adjust at speed, and, coupled with GNR drivers' tendency to use traditional driving

techniques that were not suitable for these modern machines, led to their being regarded as 'disappointing'. The use of the same valve gear as the smaller-boilered locomotives, still with slide valves, made them quite thirsty as well.

Before the next 60 locomotives were built, between early 1905 and the end of 1908, modifications were made to the firebox, both to make it deeper and to provide room for a newly designed air-assisted screw reverser. The latter made the locomotives easier to work, and the deeper firebox had a steeper slope, which allowed coal to slide down to the front and greatly aided firing the locomotives. It was in this form that the design would be adopted for the Brighton Atlantics.

BELOW The GNR's extension of the Ivatt Atlantic design by Sir Nigel Gresley was the famous 'A1' (later 'A3') class of Pacific. His initial design in 1915 for a Pacific was simply an elongated Atlantic, complete with the extremely small cab of the Ivatt locomotives and a parallel boiler, but by the time design was finalised in 1922 the tapered boiler, the large side-window cab and the Walschearts valve gear made the lineage somewhat less visible. Another of the 1905 batch of Atlantics, by now LNER No 3300 (and destined to survive nationalisation, as BR No 62828), stands at King's Cross alongside an example of its progeny, 'A3' No 4480 *Enterprise*, on 8 May 1929. Madgwick Collection

CHAPTER 2

THE ACCIDENTAL ATLANTICS

ABOVE The locomotives initially displaced by the 'H1' Atlantics were the Stroudley Class B1 'Gladstone' 0-4-2 express locomotives. Marsh had an almost compulsive dislike of front-drive locomotives on passenger work, especially express (or 'fast') trains, and was keen to downgrade or withdraw the 'Gladstones' as quickly as possible – a task he failed to accomplish. The last of this famous class outlived his stay on the LBSCR and even the company itself, the final survivors being withdrawn as late as 1933 upon electrification of the Brighton main line. *Gladstone* itself (himself?) survives today, having been rescued for preservation by the Stephenson Locomotive Society in 1926, as described in **Chapter 11.** Madgwick Collection

The London Brighton & South Coast Railway's principal business was the carrying of passengers; the South of England has few mineral resources and little heavy industry, but it does have plenty of people, and a vast number of them work in the capital. During the latter part of the 19th century the advent of the Brighton, together with the other railways of the South of England, had led to the development of that part of London which lies to the south of the River Thames. Most Brighton runs were short, of less than 30 miles, but with many stops. The backbone of its system was the Brighton main line, but even that was just 51 miles; its longest line, to Portsmouth, extended for a shade over 88 miles, although this was more of a secondary cross-country line than a fast main line. Only the Brighton main line saw any true expresses (although the Brighton did not deign to use this term, referring only to 'fast' services), the target being to reach London within the hour, which would be met by the all-Pullman 'Pullman Limited', introduced on 2 October 1898. This ran only on Sundays, but not between July and September. After a rival company, the London & Brighton Electric Railway, made an application to Parliament in 1900 and threatened to compete with the LBSCR by building an all-electric line to Brighton, the 'Brighton Limited' (formerly the 'Pullman Limited', 'Brighton Pullman Limited' and 'Pullman Limited Express' – it had had many names!) made a record run on

26 July 1903 from the capital in 48 minutes 41 seconds, equalling the forecast electric timings and demonstrating that the LBSCR was quite able to compete. But the threat turned the company's thoughts to electrification of its own lines, even though Parliament refused to authorise the London & Brighton Electric Railway.

Frequent, lightweight trains were the rule on the Brighton. In 1904 the railway owned but one corridor carriage; independently owned Pullmans were used on the best trains. Six-wheelers were still commonplace, although the passengers – most of whom were what we would today call commuters – weren't too worried about moving around in a train that would carry them for only an hour or so; they were much more interested in being able to sit down. (*Plus ça change!*) To power these trains the LBSCR Locomotive Department, initially under the leadership of the famous William Stroudley (CME from 1870 to 1889) and later of his former protégé, Robert James Billinton (Stroudley's assistant at Brighton Works from 1870 to 1874 and his successor from 1890), had produced a series of tank engines with four- or six-coupled wheels, which together made up more than 75% of the company's passenger-locomotive stock as at 7 November 1904, when Robert Billinton died suddenly, at the age of 59.

Billinton had followed the standards laid down by Stroudley (who is often credited as the father of the standardisation of locomotive design) and built a number of

BELOW Robert Billinton's Class B4 4-4-0s were the Brighton's largest passenger locomotives when Marsh took over following Billinton's death in 1905. They were an extension of his earlier and smaller 'B2' and 'B3' designs and had command of the principal fast trains without entirely superseding the 'Gladstones'. In celebration of the Entente Cordiale No 54 *Empress* was temporarily named *La France* for nine days in 1905 in order to work Royal specials in connection with the visit of the French Navy's visit to Portsmouth. The name would later be applied to No 39, the only Marsh Atlantic to bear a name in LBSCR days. *Madgwick Collection*

RIGHT A picture summing up the crisis that brought two successive Brighton locomotive superintendents to their knees – lines of locomotives in the countryside, awaiting a slot in the Brighton Works overhaul programme. In the Edwardian era up to 150 locomotives would be held like this, representing an astonishing 30% or so of the total stock. This line-up of at least nine locomotives rusting away on the Ashurst spur near East Grinstead in 1906 includes three 'B2s' (that nearest the camera being No 51 *Wolferton*, just five years old) as well as Stoudley 'E1' No 146 *Havre* and Billinton 'E4s' Nos 516 *Rustington* (also just five years old), 476 *Beeding* and 478 *Newick*, along with an unidentified 'C1' goods engine and another 'E4'.

Madgwick Collection

classes which extended the Stroudley design principles. His most notable deviation was the design of his express passenger 4-4-0 locomotives of Classes B2 and B4, 24 of the former (plus a solitary 'B3') and 33 of the latter being the most up-to-date types of locomotive on the Brighton; one of the 'B4s', No 70 *Holyrood*, had been responsible for the record run in July 1903. The principal departure from Stroudley practice lay in the use of a leading four-wheel bogie, Stroudley having used no leading unpowered wheels on any of his locomotive types with the exception of his 2-2-2 express locomotives, these being replaced by the 'B2s' and 'B4s'. *His* principal express type was the 'B1' ('Gladstone') 0-4-2, of which 36 (the last built as recently as 1890) were still on top-link work in 1904, Billinton's 4-4-0s having proven to be something of a mixed bag.

The 'B2s', dating from 1895, had proven entirely incapable of supplanting the 'Gladstones', and this had led to the larger 'B3' (a 'B2' with a larger boiler) and then, in the summer of 1899, to the 'B4s', which would at least equal the 'Gladstones'. Twenty 'B4s' were authorised in August 1899, but only two had been built by January 1900, with work on the third one suspended, these three replacing (and utilising material bought for) three cancelled 'B2s' or 'B3s'. This was the tip of an iceberg which would have a direct bearing on the Brighton Atlantic story.

The iceberg was Brighton Works. Built on

a cramped site just outside the LBSCR's main station and headquarters, this was bursting at the seams. Maintenance backlogs were building up, and there simply was not the capacity to erect the rest of the new locomotives. The third 'B4' eventually emerged in May 1900, having been erected at weekends by staff on overtime pay! This *débâcle* had two principal consequences. The first was that an order was placed with Sharp, Stewart & Co of Manchester for a further 20

Class B4s (the initial pair having proven a major advance over their 'B2' predecessors), Brighton Works being authorised to build a further five during 1901. The contractor-built machines appeared from June to October, but the five Brighton locomotives, for which frames had been cut, were soon cancelled, there being still no capacity (the frames being placed in store), and the Sharp, Stewart order was increased to 25. The repair backlog having been brought under control, yet

another attempt was made to build further locomotives and, taking a year to do it, Brighton turned out a final five 'B4s' which emerged between June and September 1902. Happily, the class proved to be as good as the 'B2s' were bad, other than having a worrying tendency to suffer frame fractures.

The second consequence of the maintenance backlog was that the Brighton directors again considered whether to relocate the works – 'again' inasmuch as a plan had been drawn up to move it to Horley (just to the east of the main line) as early as 1841, a matter of months after it had been established at Brighton! Stroudley re-evaluated the plan in the 1870s but merely moved non-locomotive work to Newhaven (Marine Works) and carriage repairs and paint shops to a new facility nearby but still on the east side of the main line at Brighton. However, once again, nothing was done about it and the resumption of construction of the 'B4' class probably gave

a false impression that the crisis had passed. It certainly looked a lot better, as there were no long lines of locomotives awaiting attention. But that was also a false impression, as they had simply been parked 'off-site', as it were, in sidings at Horsted Keynes, East Grinstead and Horley! Into this maelstrom came Douglas Earle Marsh.

Probably it was the stress of managing Brighton Works that took a toll on the health of Robert Billinton. In October 1904, having visited him, one of the directors reported that his health was 'very grave'. Billinton had agreed that he could no longer carry out his duties and offered his resignation, effective at the end of the year. This was accepted at the Board meeting of 19 October 1904, after which the directors advertised the position, applicants being asked to attend an interview on 9 November. Two days before that, Robert Billinton died.

Marsh had had an earlier acquaintance with Brighton when, aged 16, he went to Brighton College for the last two years of his schooling, from 1878. During that time he may have visited Brighton Works, then at the height of the Stroudley era, with locomotive No 40 (a diminutive Class A1 0-6-0 tank, commonly known as a 'Terrier') winning a Gold Medal at the Paris Exhibition of 1878 for the excellence of its workmanship. This may have impressed the directors, who appointed him Chief Mechanical Engineer with effect from 1 January 1905. Already in turmoil, Brighton Works thus had to manage for nearly two months without a chief engineer.

One of Marsh's first actions upon arriving at Brighton was to modify Stroudley's system of locomotive classification, making it similar to that of the GNR, starting at 'A1' for the 'Terriers' and running up to 'G' for the Stroudley 2-2-2 passenger locomotives; it is these classifications that are used in this book. With the 'Gs' finishing the sequence, the first Marsh locomotives would logically be the 'H' class. But before we examine them in detail, yet more background information about Marsh himself is required, to explain how they came about.

In between his stays in Brighton Marsh had had an interesting career which was to shape his approach to locomotive design and have a direct influence on his designs for the Brighton, of which all but one (a goods engine, Class C3) would have a leading four-wheel bogie. After he finished his time at Brighton College he went to University College London, where he studied various engineering and geological matters on a three-year course, following which he obtained a position at Swindon Works on the Great Western Railway under William Dean's superintendency; this was right at the end of the broad-gauge era, which, as explained earlier, taught him the advantages of a wide firebox. Here he became a draughtsman and, in May

1889, at the age of 27, Assistant Works Manager. In this post he had some uncomfortable working relationships, so he must have been pleased to accept an appointment at Doncaster as Henry Ivatt's Chief Assistant Mechanical Engineer and Doncaster Works Manager with effect from 1 January 1896.

On 13 April 1895, just before Marsh left Swindon, a pair of Great Western Class 3521 0-4-4 tanks, rebuilt from broad-gauge 'convertible' 0-4-2 tanks, were working an express train on the newly re-laid Cornish main line, whence they had been banished after proving to be 'prone to falling off the rails when it was least convenient' (*An Outline of Great Western Locomotive Practice*, H Holcroft, Ian Allan Ltd (p60/61 1971 edition). This proved to be a somewhat prophetic report, as when they were approaching Doublebois (near Bodmin Road) they ran straight off the road, causing complete mayhem and injuries to 15 passengers. The track had been damaged by the locomotives of the preceding train, also headed by a pair of these locomotives. This made Marsh very wary of employing front-coupled locomotives on fast trains, something that was to be reinforced a couple of years later when a Drummond Class M7 0-4-4 tank of the LSWR also came to grief on a West Country express, near Tavistock. Following these accidents both types of locomotive were taken off express duties, the GWR '3521s' being rebuilt as 4-4-0s. Significantly, at this time front-coupled locomotives were employed on almost all trains on the Brighton, the 'B2s', 'B3' and 'B4s' being the only locomotives not built to this layout.

At Doncaster Marsh enjoyed an extremely good working relationship with Ivatt and was closely involved with the design, construction and maintenance of the new Atlantics. It has often been suggested that a chief engineer had little to do with the actual design of locomotives, being more of a manager, and that most design work was down to the draughtsmen, so it is seems reasonable to assume that Marsh made a significant contribution to the design of the 'Ivatt' Atlantics. During this time he travelled widely to see what was being developed in mainland Europe, and in Hungary he became interested in the early use of petrol-driven rail vehicles, upon his return persuading Ivatt to build some petrol railcars for use on the

Hatfield branch in an attempt to reduce costs. In Germany he 'discovered' the Schmidt superheater, which had been created as early as 1890 but not used in steam locomotives until 1898 (experimentally) and 1902 (in series production of the Prussian 'S 4' type), and became one of its earliest advocates. Both these experiences would have a bearing upon the Brighton Atlantics.

Another factor in the story leading up to the birth of the Brighton Atlantics was the course of the Brighton company's business in the early part of the Edwardian era. From the turn of the century the rise of street tramways had severely undermined suburban traffic. As we have already noted, in 1903 the Board decided that electrification was the solution and, with its eye on complete electrification of its services to Brighton itself, decided to use an overhead wiring system energised at 6,600V AC. Planning and installation of this for the first line, that from Victoria to London Bridge via the South London line, would absorb finance and manpower for six years, the line being energised in 1909. This would, as is well known with regard to the later widespread electrification of the Southern Railway, be something of a constraint upon steam-locomotive policy and funding. Certainly Brighton Works' troubles became worse rather than better during this period, and reorganisation must have been uppermost in the minds of the directors when they appointed Marsh to the post of CME, his experiences at both Swindon and Doncaster as Works Manager seemingly making him the ideal candidate.

As Marsh would soon discover, Brighton Works was faced with a backlog of repairs, and the drawing office staff were engaged on detailed plans for electrification; there was also an urgent need for new express locomotives to haul the new, heavier rolling stock that by this time was starting to trickle into service, whilst suburban traffic was under threat and longer-distance commuting was on the rise. Another threat to passenger traffic was manifesting itself outside the Metropolitan suburban area, in places such as Brighton itself and Worthing, where early charabancs and local tramways, coupled with increasing staff costs, were undermining the economics of running local trains. Consequently, in common with other

ATLANTIC EXPRESS ENGINE, L.B. & S.C.R. 534.

By The Locomotive Publishing Company, Ltd., London, E.C.

railways in the South of England, the LBSCR was forced to look at ways of providing cheaper trains. Steam railmotors – self-contained trains – appeared to offer one solution, and the Brighton joined the LSWR in providing a pair of these to work the Southsea branch. In view of the crisis at Brighton Works it was perhaps fortunate that Dugald Drummond on the LSWR carried out all the design work and that the locomotives were built at Nine Elms and the carriage portions at Eastleigh, where final assembly was undertaken. Introduced to traffic in April 1903, they were a complete failure, despite various 'improvements'. The Brighton decided that it had to look elsewhere for lower-cost trains, and this was another area in which Marsh would be able to bring his expertise to bear, notably in terms of his knowledge of internal-combustion engines in rail use. Indeed this would become one of his early priorities – another reason he would have little time to devote to organising a brand-new design of express steam locomotive.

A number of authorities have stated that Marsh arrived at Brighton with a complete set of drawings of the Ivatt Atlantics, which if

true would be an early example of industrial espionage! This seems unlikely, but he must have been working on them during the previous year, as that was the time that the improvements to the latter had been made to good effect. What is known is that, having shown illustrations of the Ivatt Atlantics and explained that they could handle faster trains, even with a weight increase of 33%, Marsh was authorised by the Brighton Engine Stock Committee on 22 March 1905 to prepare specifications and drawings for five new locomotives 'of a more powerful type than those at present in use on the railway' (a reference to the 'B4s'). The decision was ratified by the Board the following week. At this time the Ivatt Atlantics were considered the apogee of modern British motive power, and the opportunity to acquire some must have been a major factor in the decision to authorise Marsh to provide them, as the time thus freed up would enable him to concentrate on matters the directors regarded as more pressing.

It might be argued that the Atlantic format was not ideally suited to the short runs with a number of stops which were common on the

ABOVE The first Brighton Atlantic, No 37, as built, illustrated in *The Railway Magazine* of November 1906. Ian Allan Library

Brighton system and that a 4-6-0 might have a more logical extension of the 4-4-0 format, with that type's greater surefootedness on starting. But it was Marsh's knowledge of and confidence in the Ivatt Atlantics (as well as his own direct input into their design and development) that won the day and changed the course of Brighton steam-locomotive practice.

Having obtained his authorisation Marsh lost no time in asking his former employer for copies of the working drawings of the latest Class C1 Atlantics (which rather disproves the notion that he arrived at Brighton with them) and then, having made a few alterations in red ink, sending them off to tender in early April. This, obviously, would be much quicker than it would have been had a new design been started from scratch. Thus, as a result of the accident of Billinton's incapacity and death, the accident at Doublebois and the urgent need for some new express locomotives, the 'H1' Atlantics came into being.

CHAPTER 3

COPYCATS – THE 'H1s'

ABOVE Standing outside London's Victoria station alongside 'B2' 4-4-0 No 317 *Gerald Loder* of 1895, No 41, the final example of the first class of Brighton Atlantics, shows the enormous advances in locomotive size in barely a decade. The 'B2' would shortly be rebuilt by Marsh with a much larger boiler. Madgwick Collection

The best (lowest) quote for building the Atlantics came from James Kitson, of Leeds, and was accepted on 19 April 1905, exactly four weeks after authorisation was given – an indication of how speed was of the essence. In some respects it was a stopgap solution as a result of the various factors that had led to the order, which was for just five locomotives – barely sufficient to undertake two or three diagrams per day. They would, however, give the Brighton's publicity department something to crow about. Suddenly, the LBSCR, an oft-overlooked 'little' railway, would be at the forefront of locomotive development in an era when the steam locomotive was at the cutting edge of technology as the railways enjoyed their 'Golden Age' in the final decade before the Great War changed everything.

The first three locomotives were initially classed as 'B5', but upon the arrival of No 40 in February 1906 they all became Class H (and then H1 from 1 January 1907). They cost £3,950 each (less £45 for being delivered in grey primer rather than the Stroudley 'improved engine green' initially specified), and delivery was to be by September, with a premium of £10 per week payable in the event of early delivery. The latter was not to be, as the first locomotive did not arrive until 10 December 1905, the other four following within two months. Upon arrival they were

painted in a new 'burnt umber' livery and numbered from 37 to 41, but, in a break with Brighton tradition, they bore no names. Thus they stood out as modern and imposing locomotives, albeit somewhat alien to those who worshipped the Stroudley tradition. But it was precisely that, of course, from which Marsh was trying to break away!

The principal 'red ink' alterations (ignoring cosmetic changes) to the Ivatt design were as follows:

> Boiler pressure increased to 200 lb sq in (from 175 lb sq in)
> Piston stroke increased to 26in (24in)
> Piston bore of 18½in (Nos 37/8) or 19in thereafter (18¾in)
> Frame length increased to 34ft 4½in (from 33ft 1¼in)
> A firebox depth (below boiler centreline) of 5ft 1¾in at the front, 4ft 7½in at the rear
> Westinghouse air brakes
> Larger, square cabs with clerestories

Tenders were a modified version of the design used by Billinton for the 'B4s'.

Cosmetic alterations lay in the shape of the running boards, which were continuous over the cylinders (although still dropping behind them and rising again before the driving-

wheel splashers), as well as of the chimney and dome, while the fitting of bogie brakes and various standard Brighton fixtures such as buffers and lamp-irons also subtly altered their appearance. What is perhaps more surprising is what was not changed: cab-front windows, safety-valve casing and type (Ramsbottom), handrails, buffer-beam, footsteps and smokebox door – although the hinge-straps were different!

It is worth considering what other railways had built for express passenger work by the time the 'H1s' first appeared. Today we look back at them and think of them as quite small and dainty when we compare them to the later Pacific types that ruled the rails, but in 1905 there were no Pacifics and very few express passenger 4-6-0s on British metals; most 4-6-0s were for mixed-traffic or goods duties, and indeed the first British 4-6-0s were the 'Jones Goods' of the Highland Railway. Many people will be familiar with the big Churchward standard designs of the early Edwardian era, but on 10 December 1905 the Great Western Railway had only two prototype Churchward 4-6-0s (Nos 98 and 100), one prototype Atlantic (No 171, which was converted *from* a 4-6-0) and a series of 13 production Atlantics and seven 4-6-0s, plus three more Atlantics imported from France. Thus even Churchward at this time had nearly twice as many Atlantics as 4-6-0s. (The Dean 4-6-0s were goods engines).

Only seven other companies had put express passenger 4-6-0s into service by the end of 1905. The NER had already tried and rejected them, replacing 15 Worsdell-designed Classes S and S1 4-6-0s by 10 Class V Atlantics, as the 4-6-0s were insufficiently free-running. The GCR had in 1903 experimented with two Class 8C 4-6-0s together with two similar (Class 8B) Atlantics – and had gone on to build more Atlantics but no more '8Cs'. The Caledonian had two Class 49s, which were a great disappointment. The LNWR had five 'Experiments', designed by George Whale, although the subsequent class would eventually number 105 and might reasonably be considered a success. The Glasgow & South

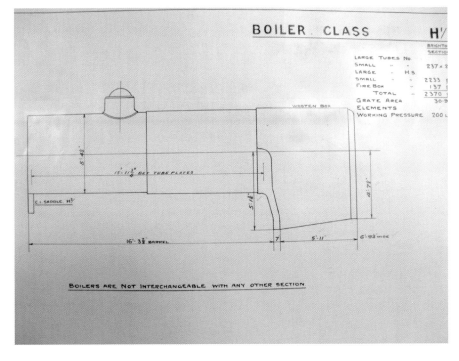

LEFT 'H1' boiler diagram. The principal difference from the Ivatt boiler is the depth of the firebox. NRM

ABOVE AND BELOW Comparative views of an Ivatt 'C1' in later life (as **LNER No 4444**) and Brighton 'H1' No 37 as built, showing how they were, essentially, one and the same design. The bogie brakes on the Brighton locomotive are just discernible. Madgwick Collection, Noodle Books

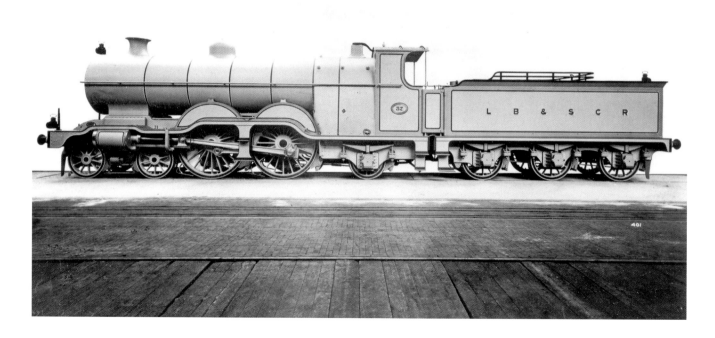

RIGHT No 39 is seen alongside Hove Cliftonville Junction splitting signals whilst on test in 1906 in a very posed photograph. There are no windows or portholes in the somewhat crude indicator shelter so the bowler-hatted engineers would have had to stand like this when the locomotive was working if they needed to see where they were! *Madgwick Collection*

Western Railway had seven (and was building more) of its '381' class – possibly the second-most-successful 4-6-0 class of its time (Churchward's machines being by far the most successful). Finally, Dugald Drummond of the LSWR had built five ungainly Class F13s, which were as poor in service as they looked and, with 6ft driving wheels, could not really be counted as express passenger locomotives. His brother, Peter (who was one of three others, besides Marsh, to apply for the open position at Brighton), had designed a series of passenger 4-6-0s for the Highland Railway in 1900 which, with 5ft 9in drivers, were even less 'express' locomotives than his brother's, albeit much more successful. And that was the sum total of express passenger 4-6-0s in service at the end of 1905 as the first Brighton Atlantic was delivered – a mere 39, compared to more than four times that number of Atlantics. Whereas 4-6-0s were regarded as plodders, Atlantics were considered fleet of foot, and the Brighton locomotives were particularly 'cutting edge', being effectively part of the most successful Atlantic 'family' of all.

The first of the significant mechanical differences from the Ivatt engines, the increased stroke, was achieved by turning the connecting rod pins one inch off-centre whilst retaining the coupling rod cranks at 12 inches as per the Ivatts. (Perhaps it was easier to do that than completely re-draw the plans!) Equally significant was the change in piston diameter, the cylinders of the first two being bored to 18½in, ¼in less than the Ivatts (presumably to compensate for the increased stroke) but increased to ¼in *larger* with No 39. Although numerically small, the increase in diameter follows a geometric curve and expressed as a percentage increase equates to a 7% increase over the Ivatts' swept volume for the 18½in cylinders and nearly 10% (actually 9.76%) for the 19in cylinders. It was said that the Ivatts were under-cylindered, but I have never heard that said of the Marsh locomotives. Perhaps he

had learned a thing or two at Doncaster! Nominally, according to the tractive-effort calculations, the Marsh engines were 26% 'more powerful' than the Ivatts, although tractive effort is somewhat disregarded today. For the record, the 'H1s' could produce 19,028lb ft, the Ivatts 15,649lb ft – but there certainly was not that degree of difference in their performance. The third significant mechanical change was the increased boiler pressure, 200psi being quite rare in 1905, but necessary to feed the bigger cylinders.

The changes meant that the Marsh locomotives were a little more lively than the Ivatts and had extra torque in order to combat the steep climbs away from some LBSCR stations, notably Grosvenor Bank, virtually from the platform ends at Victoria, and the long climbs in both directions over (and through) the South Downs. They did, of course, suffer from the problem inherent in all locomotives with a trailing carrying axle, that of 'sitting back' on that axle and losing

traction on starting – a tendency that would influence Churchward's decision to standardise on 4-6-0s after running both types in service for some time.

Other than being pressed to a higher pressure the boiler was essentially the same as that of the Ivatt machines and, at 5ft 6in diameter, was one of the largest on the railways at that time; even Drummond's seemingly massive locomotives had a boiler only one inch greater in diameter. The grate area was the same in both types of Atlantic, at 30.95sq ft, although Marsh had modified the slope of the grate even further than had Ivatt in his second series. (This marked similarity would be the foundation stone of the project to build a 12th Marsh Atlantic in the 21st century.) The heating surfaces were slightly less than those of the Ivatts, having 2,318sq ft in the boiler and 136½sq ft in the firebox (comparable figures for the Ivatts being 2,359sq ft and 141sq ft respectively).

ABOVE No 39 is again seen with the indicator shelter – this time with no-one looking over the top! – on a Portsmouth train between Sutton and Cheam.
Madgwick Collection

BELOW The first Brighton Atlantic in service on an Arun Valley-line train at Sutton. The line was not a usual route for these locomotives in their early days, so this may well be a test run; no date is recorded for the photograph, but it must have been taken *c*1908, judging from 'raspberries' (the intertwined company initials, which were applied only upon first repaint) on the splashers. *Madgwick Collection*

ABOVE Possibly the most successful Atlantics, yet easily the shortest-lived in this form, were the Churchward locomotives of the Great Western Railway. One (No 171) was converted from a 4-6-0 in 1904, and 13 were built alongside his standard 'Saint' 4-6-0s so that Churchward could compare the two layouts. The 4-6-0 won, all the Atlantics being converted to 4-6-0s in 1912/3. No 180 was built in 1905 and named *Coeur de Lion* in 1907. Renumbered 2980, it was rebuilt as a 4-6-0 in January 1913. Madgwick Collection

Surprisingly, in view of their extra length, the Marsh locomotives were actually some 1 ton 6cwt *lighter* than their progenitors (which weighed 68 tons 6cwt), although that might be due to differing parameters used to calculate the weight. It might also be explained, at least in part, by another altered feature: the air for the reverser came from the Westinghouse brake pump, whereas the Ivatts had to have a special air pump for that purpose only.

One visible difference between members of the 'H1' class was the length of the cab roof. The roof provided on the first three proved inadequate so the last two had extended roofs. It cannot have been too serious an issue, as it was not until after the Grouping that the first three were altered to match. The pioneer, No 37, also differed in very a minor way in that its works plate was affixed to the frames ahead of the smokebox until the locomotive was fully painted, whereupon the plate was moved to the frames ahead of the coupled wheel splashers, where Nos 38-41 had theirs from new.

However much they might have appeared to be yet more Ivatt Atlantics, to the Brighton the 'H1s' were new and something to be

ABOVE The celebrated No 39, considered to be 'a good one', posed early in its career but, again, after its first repaint. The bogie brakes are well lit in this undated photograph. The Brighton had an exceedingly complicated system of route codes and headlamp positions which necessitated tall and duplicated lamp irons and involved the use of square route indicators as well as the more familiar discs. Ian Allan Library

proud of. Their arrival gave the company the powerful locomotives it needed to improve services, but there was no immediate change in the train schedules, giving the crews time to get used to the new locomotives. Until the end of the Great War crews were normally allocated individual locomotives and thus took great pride in 'their engine'. The corollary of this was that it did not take the regular crews of the Atlantics long to get to know their new mounts, despite their having so many 'foreign' parts and features as well as the great increase in power over the previous 'B4s'. All five were allocated to Brighton shed from new and took over haulage of the principal trains, including the Sundays-only Pullman, the 'Brighton Limited'.

By the mid-1900s the Edwardian era was in full bloom, and ostentatious living was an obvious expression of the 'Age of Elegance'. On the railways this manifested itself in even more elaborate liveries and, more importantly, internal fittings of carriage

stock. The prosperity of the upper classes was expressed in high living, which included moving to the seaside during the summer months, as it wasn't 'done' to remain in London at that time. They travelled to and from Brighton on the LBSCR and helped the company with their increased patronage, but of course they expected those improved facilities. However, all was not well on the Brighton, and 1907 proved to be a difficult year for the company. Receipts were down yet expenditure on a wide range of capital projects was high, including the need to improve the services to meet this demand.

Shortly before Marsh took over the post of Locomotive, Carriage & Wagon Superintendent, Alfred Panter, the Carriage & Wagon Works Manager, had introduced eight-wheel bogie carriages to improve normal main-line services, many of which still included in their formation at least one Pullman car. Ongoing improvements were being made to the main line, which had benefited enormously from the construction in 1899 of the Quarry line, to avoid a bottleneck at Redhill. This moved the bottleneck further south, which matter was addressed from 1906, the 16-mile stretch of line between Earlswood and Three Bridges being quadrupled over the ensuing three years. This was another massively expensive project which absorbed a large part of the Brighton's capital spending budget.

One of Marsh's priorities was to reorganise Brighton Works, the logical solution being to remove the Carriage & Wagon Works to a new site altogether. On 20 February 1907 the Board approved the construction of a new

works at Lancing, but the severe downturn in receipts led to a scaling-back of the plan – Lancing Works would not be completed until 1912. Thus Brighton's reorganisation was also delayed, and the backlog of repairs once again began to grow out of control, the situation being exacerbated by the fact that locomotive construction had recommenced in 1906 and would continue through 1907. The construction of a new boiler shop (or, rather, rearrangement of the existing one) also slowed matters, and Marsh's somewhat difficult nature made labour relations at the Works extremely strained.

The combination of more urgent priorities thus ensured that 'H1s' remained the only modern express locomotives on the rapidly changing Brighton system. No 39, which had the larger cylinders, seems to have been the best of the five and was used on a special run on 30 June 1907 with seven heavy Pullman cars and two vans (total gross weight of around 240 tons) to run from Victoria to Brighton in 51 minutes 48 seconds, reaching a maximum speed of 86½mph near Wivelsfield. The full journey is described by Donald

Bradley as an 'epic' run in his RCTS book about Brighton locomotives, *Locomotives of the L.B.&S.C.R., Volume 3* 1974).

Curiously, the Atlantics were not fitted with steam heating until October 1908, in preparation for a major timetable change which came into effect on 8 November, when, following the line improvements which made the main line four-track almost as far as Balcombe Tunnel, the 'Brighton Limited' was promoted to daily operation and renamed the 'Southern Belle'. The new Atlantics were the prime choice for working this train, which

BELOW No 40 enters East Croydon station with the 'Brighton Limited', most probably in early 1906 as the Pullman Cars of the train are still in dark mahogany brown rather than the umber and cream introduced later that year. Note the 'Pullman Pup' six-wheel dynamo and luggage van at the head of the train and the immaculate burnished buffers and smokebox fittings of the locomotive. In the siding to the right is one of the Stroudley 'D' tanks.
Madgwick Collection

worked two round trips per day. For this the Pullman Car Co built its first carriages in Great Britain, having earlier established a works at Preston Park, a little way up the Brighton main line north of the Locomotive Works. This cemented ties with the LBSCR, already the most enthusiastic user of Pullman cars, which hitherto had been built in the USA and assembled in Great Britain, initially at Derby and later at Preston Park. It will not escape the reader's notice that the enthusiastic use of Pullmans effectively provided the company with new coaching stock which it had neither to build nor finance! The new cars set the standard which all subsequent British Pullmans would follow and were exceptional in their lavish fittings – including, of course, steam heating. They were consequently very heavy, riding on six-wheel bogies, and the new 'Southern Belle' set of seven cars, delivered just in time for the start of the new services, was a wonder of the age, the train being promoted in early publicity brochures as 'the finest train in the world'.

Cecil J. Allen, in one of his early 'Locomotive Practice and Performance' articles for *The Railway Magazine* of August 1912, reported that he had by that time travelled more than 3,000 miles behind Brighton Atlantics – quite a feat on a railway with a main line of just 51 miles! More importantly, he stated: 'I have never known a minute to have been lost in the running, which certainly speaks well for the engines and their drivers.' He described three runs behind the 'H1s' which showed that they could run fast and well – nearly 80mph on a line as crowded as the Brighton main line was quite something at that time. The first run featured No 39 with its regular driver J. Cox departing Victoria on the 'Southern Belle', now with the new carriages weighing 290 tons, a 20% increase over the American-built cars. Despite a slightly late start, a permanent-way restriction and a brief signal check, Brighton was reached on time, the locomotive reaching a maximum speed of 77½mph, once again near Wivelsfield. In the opposite direction No 41, with driver J. Tompsett, on the 1.20pm up express reached a

ABOVE No 41 was photographed near Norbury on the 11.00am 'Sunday Pullman'. The Pullman Cars have now been repainted in the more familiar umber and cream livery which the Pullman Company adopted during 1906, a variation on the Brighton company's own livery. With the Atlantics bearing Marsh's umber livery the whole ensemble was one of the finest and most prestigious Edwardian trains of all.
Madgwick Collection

maximum of 74mph, while, on the lightweight (110-ton) 8.30pm down train from Victoria a maximum of 79 was achieved, this time by No 37 approaching the stop at Haywards Heath. By contrast, Bradley records that in 1909/10 the 8.45am from Brighton boasted a 13-coach formation (including three Pullmans) weighing 392 tons. These figures show that the locomotives were on top of the job and must have still had power to spare. The Edwardian 'toffs' must surely have been quietly pleased with them.

ABOVE AND BELOW Two photographs of No 39, the first on the Pullmans entering East Croydon with the 'square disc' indicating a train scheduled to run via the new Quarry Line and the second showing it on a Mid-Sussex line train at Mitcham Common forming the 11.35am train from London Victoria to Portsmouth. Again these are undated, but are probably between 1906 and 1908. Note the tall lampirons employed by the Brighton, the second photograph showing the stacked lamps very clearly. Both - Madgwick Collection

ABOVE 'H1' Atlantic No 38 is seen on a matched rake of Brighton corridor stock near Mitcham Common on the 11.35am London Victoria to Portsmouth train.

E. T. Vise, Madgwick Collection

BELOW Still unnamed and sporting a cast numberplate, No 39 is seen adorned with elaborate decorations in order to haul a Royal train carrying King George V and Queen Mary from Portsmouth after their return on 4 February 1912 from a three-month tour of British India. As a cost-cutting measure, from October 1908 the cab-side cast numberplates were gradually removed from the 'H1s' and substituted with painted numerals.

Madgwick Collection

FAILURE – THE 'I1s', 'I2s' AND 'I4s'

ABOVE The second of the 'mongrel' Marsh Atlantic tanks, No 2, looks very elegant at the head of a rake of Brighton close-coupled suburban stock, the absence of the ampersand from the company initials revealing that the photograph was taken sometime after 1908. Sadly, serious shortcomings belied these locomotives' good looks and would appear to have arisen from the requirement to fit a very short firebox in order to reuse components from old Stroudley locomotives; the resultant 7ft 7in coupled wheelbase was extremely restrictive, as the inside valve gear used some of the space between the wheels and left just 5ft 8¼in for the firebox, an effect not seen on the donor locomotives, which were front-coupled. Madgwick Collection

The term 'Atlantic' is normally associated with tender engines, but in Great Britain there were rather more tank-engine designs featuring the 4-4-2 wheel layout, so, besides the rather better-remembered tender engines, it seems logical to examine the Atlantic tanks which Marsh introduced to the Brighton.

Marsh's first all-new design for the Brighton was a complete failure, although it was a very simple 0-6-0 goods engine. Ten Class C3s were produced, built at Brighton between March and November 1906. They play no further part in our story of the Brighton Atlantics, other than, rather worryingly, to set the scene for Marsh's first *original* Atlantic design, the 'I1' 4-4-2T.

In the wake the failure of the 'C3s' the equal failure of the Class I1 tanks must have come as something of a shock to the Brighton, which was basking in the glory of the highly effective 'H1s'. The 'I1s', like the tender engines, had their roots in Ivatt locomotives on the GNR, in this case the latter's Class C2 (LNER Class C12), and it has been suggested that Marsh

once again obtained copies of Doncaster drawings to modify, although there is no evidence of this and they were only similar in that they were 4-4-2 tanks. Be that as it may, the Ivatt tanks, dating from 1898 and following the 'Klondykes' in the GNR's classification system, were extremely successful, 60 being built by 1907, whereas the Marsh locomotives were a total failure. Curiously, by 1903 the GNR 'C2' tanks were effectively obsolete as they were having difficulty coping with heavier trains, prompting Ivatt to introduce the Class L1 (LNER R1) 0-8-2 tanks; when these proved disappointing he produced his Class N1 0-6-2 tanks in 1907.

Although Pacific tanks would feature later, at this stage of his design career Marsh's locomotives were quite small and thus had only two driven axles, notwithstanding that the 'E4' and 'E5' 0-6-2 radial tanks were very successful in the secondary passenger role, having the security of six driven wheels which made them quick off the mark from the frequent stops of such services. It is now

time to explain why the 'I1' design was regarded as a failure.

Marsh continued to maintain his antipathy toward front-coupled locomotives (in 1905 he converted a number of the inherited Stroudley and Billinton front-coupled tanks from 0-6-0s to 2-4-0s and from 0-6-2s to 2-4-2s by removing the front coupling-rod sections), his solution being to provide his designs with a front bogie, and

BELOW Reputedly the basis of the 'I1' design, Ivatt's 'C2' (LNER 'C12') class does not seem to have had a poor reputation. Not hobbled by the requirement to restrict the firebox dimensions to accommodate old parts, these locomotives led useful lives, the last being retired as late as 1958. This is LNER No 4520 near Bartlow, Cambridgeshire, on the 3.20pm train from Saffron Walden in the depths of World War 2, on 9 September 1943. Dating from 1900, this locomotive, latterly BR No 67375, would last until April 1955. *Madgwick Collection*

ABOVE A side view of the fourth 'mongrel', showing the original condition of these short-wheelbase locomotives as built. The driving wheels, retrieved from Stroudley 'D Tank' No 11, had wrought-iron centres with rectangular-section spokes and square-ended balance weights.
Ian Allan Library

his first tank-engine designs came out as 4-4-2s sporting 5ft 6in driving wheels. These were intended for the still rapidly growing suburban and local passenger services so were of comparatively light construction. It seems he took no note of his former mentor's design progress and actually reversed it!

In Marsh's opinion the old Stroudley 'D1' tank and 'D2' mixed traffic 0-4-2 locomotives were obsolete and in need of replacement, despite being far from worn out; it would appear that this decision was based as much on his prejudice against front-coupled locomotives as on sound economic reasoning. Marsh was at this time modernising the best of the earlier types by re-boilering them – a simpler and quicker process than building new locomotives. Nevertheless, in the context

of a massive backlog of repairs, building new had the advantage that existing locomotives could remain in traffic until their replacements had been built. Unfortunately, although Marsh was authorised to design and build 30 new tanks engines in 1906 it was stipulated that reuse was to be made of parts such as the driving wheels and coupling rods of the locomotives to be replaced, which somewhat negated the latter point.

Of the 30 'I1s' planned only 20 were built, and only the second batch of 10 had the inherited parts. This meant that the two batches had different coupled wheelbases, although the overall wheelbase remained the same, at 28ft 11½in. The wholly new engines, numbered 595-604, had an 8ft 9in coupled wheelbase, the 'mongrels', Nos 1-10, 7ft 7in. One oddity was that, as built, the final two locomotives were recorded as being ½in shorter than the earlier machines, although in later years they mysteriously 'gained' the extra length when converted to 'I1X' specification; Bradley records the initial reduction in length as having been 'accidental'. The parts reused in Nos 1-10 came from Stroudley 0-4-2s Nos 9, 8, 4, 11, 310, 22, 313, 311, 309 and 312 respectively.

The new locomotives were basically sound, incorporating the cylinder and valve-gear design of the GNR 'C2s'. Also incorporated was a copy of the GNR condensing system, introduced in the hope of reducing running costs, due to the perpetual poverty of the Brighton company. The boiler design could be traced back to the Stroudley-era Class G type, which had been the basis for the boiler used on the very successful 'E' series of 0-6-2 tanks. Failure came in the design of the firebox and the implementation of the condensing system, the locomotives having very poor draughting and boiler front-end design.

In view of the re-boilering he was undertaking on older classes and of his previous experience of boiler work at Doncaster, which had been one of his fortés, Marsh should have known what was required, but the 'I1' firebox and grate were too small for the new locomotives and lacked a device – common on condenser-fitted locomotives, which often suffering from poor steaming – to increase the draught and thereby improve steaming. As Bradley commented, 'No matter how they were thrashed or skilfully fired, the result was the same – pitiful.' They were also unpleasant to work, as the water tanks extended into the cab, and the condensing effect and consequent heating of the water made the cabs both hot and steamy. The first 'I1' was so bad that Marsh was prompted to add clerestory roof vents to the cabs of subsequent locomotives, improving the ventilation by adjustable louvres and lagging to the tanks, although the prototype was not so fitted retrospectively. The stipulation to reuse parts may have been partly responsible for this state of affairs, as the firebox had to be made to fit within the shorter coupled wheelbase of the second batch, restricting its size. However, in his book *Douglas Earle Marsh – His Life and Times,* Oakwood Press, 2005, Klaus Marx points out that £323 per locomotive was saved in construction costs, a significant sum to the cash-starved Brighton. The all-new machines cost £2,712 each, the 'mongrels' £2,389. It would prove a false economy.

No 595 appeared in September 1906 and was the last new Brighton locomotive to be fitted with a brass numberplate, the remainder pioneering the new, cheaper, painted numbers. Like 'H1s', the new tanks were nameless, which somehow depersonalised them; Marsh argued that the use of town names on locomotives might confuse passengers as to their destination. The first two had straight-sided smokeboxes, whilst all but the last of the remainder of the initial batch had them gently curving inwards below the centre-line in an 'S' form; No 604 and all of the second batch, Nos 1-10, had, in effect,

ABOVE No 600 on the celebrated Royal special at Epsom Downs station on Derby Day (5 June) 1907. The different pipework for the exhaust steam – highly polished and issuing from the smokebox – compared with that on Nos 1-10 may be noted. Incidentally, such was the importance of The Derby that an unsuccessful request was made in the House of Commons to adjourn for the day. It was won by Orby, an Anglo-Irish thoroughbred which ran only seven races in total, winning four of them. Curiously no LNER Pacific bore his name, but the runner-up was Wool Winder, after which an 'A3' was (incorrectly) named, while third was Slieve Gallion, a name still borne today by an Irish 4-4-0 (albeit as *Slieve Gullion*). Madgwick Collection

a circular smokebox, with just the bottom plates curved in over the frames.

Chimneys also created some different outlines. As built No 595 had a modified 'E5' chimney, but this was soon replaced by a built-up version with a cast-iron rim. Nos 596-603 had the 'E5' pattern, 2ft 3¾in tall,

while Nos 604 and 1-10 had chimneys that were nearly 1in wider at the top. Later in their careers various locomotives carried an 'E3'-pattern chimney, 2ft 9in tall. Sanding arrangements too differed between batches, the first 10 being equipped with sanding pipes in each direction for each coupled wheel, whereas the second batch had just one at the front and one at the rear of each pair.

The first five were allocated to Brighton, where Nos 595-9 were set to work on semi-fast

LEFT First of the 'mongrels' and accorded pride of place in the numbering of the LBSCR locomotive fleet, No 1 stands outside Tunbridge Wells West shed (where it was allocated from 1913), illustrating the other side of the class. The different curvature of the waist of the smokebox compared to the later series is evident. Prominent is the air pump in front of the side tank, and the locomotive has received new wheels, evidenced by the change of balance weight and rounded spokes. Alongside is one of its forebears, a 'D1', with its rather more successful condensing apparatus.
Madgwick Collection

trains. This quickly revealed their weakness and led to their being downgraded to lighter duties. Nos 600-4 went to New Cross, while the second batch were less evenly spread, Nos 1-5, 7 and 8 going to Battersea, 6 to Brighton, and 9 and 10 to New Cross. One high-profile failure served to emphasise their troubles. No 600, new in March 1907, was specially prepared in June 1907 to work a Royal special train to Epsom for The Derby, but King Edward VII, a stickler for punctuality, cannot have been too pleased that the train lost 7 minutes on the way there and 11 minutes on the return, the locomotive struggling on the 1-in-63 climb to Banstead. The Royal Train consisted of five very heavy clerestory-roofed coaches including two 12-wheeled saloons, and No 600's performance, with Marsh himself on the footplate, accompanied by Lawson Billinton (son of Robert), was possibly the reason for the cancellation of the final 10 pending a redesign. No doubt a royal complaint was made, which must have left Marsh feeling somewhat uncomfortable and Billinton reflecting that this was the man who had replaced his father!

The redesign resulted in the 1907/8-built 'I2' class, the first of these being released to traffic in the same month as the final 'I1', December 1907. Together with the 'I1s' these

TOP LEFT The 'I2s' looked more powerful than the 'I1s' on account of their larger boilers, but the same length of firebox rendered them equally ineffective. All 10 were visually identical, and the smokebox was carried on a separate saddle; the condensing apparatus was the same as for the 'I1s', with its feed into the tanks at the base. No 13 is seen before removal of its bogie brakes. H. Gordon Tidey/Madgwick Collection

BOTTOM LEFT The 'I4s' looked almost identical to the 'I2s', the superheaters and piston valves having no visible presence. The principal differences were the position of the lifting holes in the framing at the front and the provision of Klinger mechanical lubricators on the first four locomotives, this being visible just in front of the tank of Battersea-allocated No 33. This side-on view also illustrates the cab-roof ventilators in the sides of the clerestory. Ian Allan Library

10 locomotives fulfilled the authorised total of 30 and were effectively an upgrade of the 'I1' design with a slightly larger boiler, of 4ft 6in diameter rather than the 4ft 3in of the earlier machines.

Perhaps the redesign was rushed, for the new locomotive was just as bad. The driving wheelbase was lengthened, at 8ft 9in being 3in longer than the original 'I1' length, to give a total wheelbase of 30ft 7½in, the remaining increase in length resulting from setting the trailing wheels further back in the frames. Marsh, however, had not really learned anything from the 'I1' *débâcle*, as the dimensions of the firebox – 5ft 8¼in long with a 17.43sq ft grate – were identical, and the front end was the same. He did attempt to improve the steaming in one way, ordering five boilers, using saturated steam, from Brighton Works and another five with Schmidt superheaters from the North British Locomotive Co, of Glasgow, but as the latter were to be delayed by eight months a further batch of five saturated boilers was added to the Brighton order, and all 10 locomotives were built to the same design.

The situation with regard to the 'I2s' is almost unbelievable, as during the same period Marsh was also in the process of designing and organising the construction of the prototype Class I3 – although it is evident that much of the design of the new locomotives had been left to his new Chief Locomotive

ABOVE Ready for the 'off' is 'I2' No 15, suitably crowned for working the Royal Train to the 1908 Derby. Below the running-plate the cylinders for actuating the bogie brakes and the multiple pipes for fore-and-aft sanding to all driving wheels are easily seen. The race was won by a 100-to-1 outsider, Signorinetta, a victory that was met by a stunned silence from the racegoers! Madgwick Collection

Draughtsman, Basil Field, who had taken up office on 1 January 1907. The first 'I3' appeared in October 1907, two months *before* the first 'I2', and, as we shall shortly discover, proved to be as great a success as the smaller machines were failures. Perhaps Marsh was distracted by the more glamorous 'I3', but the more obvious distraction was the state of labour relations at Brighton Works, which during the summer of 1907 was reaching crisis point.

The 'I2s' were numbered 11-20, the first emerged from the works in December 1907. Field had probably had only minimal input into these, as they were really an extension of the 'I1s'. There was quite some delay before the next one – together with the second 'I3' – emerged, in March 1908, at a time when the Works reorganisation was holding up construction and repairs.

Field is credited with encouraging Marsh to try out superheating, but the latter needed little encouragement, as we have seen. The five

boilers were eventually received from North British in August 1908 and were allocated to a final series of five of the 5ft 6in tanks, initially designated 'I2 superheated' but quickly changed to 'I4' (the first 'I3' having appeared by this time). Numbered 31-5, they differed from the original 'I2s' in having piston valves to accompany the superheating. These were of 10in diameter, the cylinders being bored to 20in diameter – greater than the contemporary 'I3' and even the much larger 'H1s', so it is hardly surprising that the inadequate firebox was unable to supply sufficient steam to feed them! Field did make his mark on these engines, however, redesigning the shape of both the chimney and the safety valve, such that they were no longer of obvious Doncaster origin. The remaining 'I2s' were released to traffic throughout the spring and summer of 1908, Nos 13 and 14 in April, 15 in May, 16 in June, 17-19 in July and 20 August; the 'I4s' followed in September (31), November (32 and 33) and December (34), the class being completed by the arrival of No 35 in February 1909. Brand-new 'I2' No 15 was, somewhat alarmingly, used

on the 1908 Royal Train to The Derby, but there is no record of how it fared.

The sheds which were blessed – or, rather, cursed – with an allocation of the 'I2s' and 'I4s' were Tunbridge Wells (Nos 11 and 12), Brighton (13, 35), Eastbourne (14, 19), Battersea (15, 16 and 31-4) and New Cross (17, 18, 20).

All 35 of the small Atlantic tanks (nearly 50% of the Atlantics on the Brighton) proved to be quite extravagant on coal, Bradley reporting that they were worse than the earlier 'E5s' and the later (and larger) 'I3s'. The 'I1s' used 34.9lb per mile with loads equivalent to 8-coach trains, the 'I2s' 36.1lb (8½ coaches), and the 'I4s' 35.5lb (9 coaches); by contrast the 'E5s' used 32.7lb per mile on 10 coaches, and the 'I3s' just 30.5lb on 15 coaches. The 'I3s' will be examined in detail in the next chapter, but from the above it can be seen that not only were the small Atlantic tanks poor workhorses; they used more fuel on lighter trains than did their more powerful and larger cousins, as well as their predecessors.

The 'I4s' proved to be yet another Marsh failure. Bradley, who is quite dismissive of the

ABOVE Hopefully this is a staged shot and not evidence of a failure similar to that which befell No 600 the previous year! It is perhaps surprising that Marsh should have allowed this locomotive to be used when the first 'I3' had just been completed, but the latter had suffered a number of front-end problems and been returned to Brighton for revisions and was thus unavailable, being released from the works in May, The Derby being held on 3 June. Perhaps Marsh was just being careful! Ian Allan Library

entire group of small Atlantic tanks, states that the 'I4s' were no better (and perhaps even worse) than the 'I2s', which 'in actual performance … outshone the 'I4s', piston-valves and Schmidt superheater notwithstanding'. The latter still had the small firebox and the inadequate front end. As he also dismisses the 'I2s' as 'failing as badly as their predecessors' this really is a damning indictment of the only 'pure' Marsh locomotives built for the Brighton.

ABOVE AND BELOW The other side of an '14' (No 32) and a head-on view of No 33. These tanks were extremely elegant – an adjective which cannot really be ascribed to their immediate predecessors, the 'Radial' tanks. However, looks do not compensate for poor performance, and their lives were destined to be short. No doubt the fashionable Edwardian passengers were impressed!
Madgwick Collection, Ian Allan Library

CHAPTER 5

REDEMPTION – THE 'I3s'

ABOVE The prototype 'I3', with a chimney taller than those of the small-wheeled Atlantics, gives few visual clues to the fact that it is of an entirely different lineage and capability to that of those unfortunate machines. Here it is seen, early in its career, on the 'Southern Belle' – at the time normally the preserve of the 'H1' Atlantics – near Tooting Bec Common. This locomotive was effectively a one-off, many of its dimensions and features being modified before the subsequent locomotives were built, but it showed great promise, which was to be fulfilled in no uncertain measure. E. T. Vyse/Madgwick Collection

Reference has already been made, in a positive light, to the 'I3s', and these were without doubt the exact opposite of the 5ft 6in tanks, being a massive success.

The first 'true' Marsh express passenger engines, the 'I3s' set the tone for what would be the final phase of Brighton locomotive development. After a slightly shaky start, they incorporated all the modern refinements of the late Edwardian era, such as superheating, piston valves and well-designed steam passages, much of which, it appears, was actually down to Basil Field. Klaus Marx quotes none other than Marsh's own son, John Marsh, as telling Philip Evetts that 'Their front ends and other features were designed by Mr. Field who managed to do so when my father wasn't looking, and he should have been given the credit'. If it is right to have credited Marsh with some of the design work on the Ivatt Atlantics then it is right to ascribe much of the detail of the 'I3s' to Field, and as 'the Devil is in the details' this is where the failure of the smaller tanks is found and where the success of the larger examples must lie. However, this book is not an examination of the works of Marsh, it is the story of the Brighton Atlantics,

so the character of Marsh is relevant only in terms of how it affected the design and production of those Atlantics. If it is good management to appoint good staff then Marsh made a brilliant managerial decision to appoint Basil Field and to delegate the design of the 'I3s' to him.

The larger 4-4-2 tanks of Class I3 came about as a result of the re-boilering programme in which Marsh was engaged during 1907. Bradley records that an order had been placed with the Yorkshire Engine Co for the construction of a batch of five boilers to be fitted to the 'B4s' to increase their availability, no spare boilers having been supplied from new. They were thus basically the same as the original boilers and fully interchangeable, the objective being to speed up general overhauls. It was therefore a simple matter to divert one of these boilers to the first of a new enlarged class of tank engine, and work had started on the frames at Brighton by the time the new boilers arrived in mid-1907.

The 'I3' frames were not so much enlargements of those fitted to the smaller Atlantic tanks as lengthened versions of the

'B4' design, incorporating many 'B4' features – so much so that Bradley describes the 'I3' as 'virtually a B4 with side tanks, coal bunker and small trailing wheels in place of a tender'. The only difference other than the rear extension was in the bogie wheelbase, which, although of the Billinton pattern, was increased to 6ft 3in (from 6ft 0in). The bogie wheels were of the same diameter, 3ft 6in, and the trailing wheels 4ft 0in. Other

BELOW A closer view of the 'I3' prototype, with what appears to be a unique display of ownership on its tank sides; closer examination reveals that the 'L' has somehow disappeared! The train is of equal interest, comprising a set LNWR carriages on the celebrated 'Sunny South Express', which was to turn the 'I3' class into such icons of the Edwardian railway age. The tank engine set the pattern for future express-locomotive developments on the Brighton, disrupted only by two crises of motive power which saw the second series of Atlantic tender engines and the Maunsell 'King Arthurs' break the chain of large tank designs. Ian Allan Library

common features included the coupled wheelbase (8ft 9in), the boiler, the driving wheels (6ft 9in diameter), the cylinder and motion and, most importantly, the firebox (7ft 7in long, with a grate of 24sq ft), which had already proven itself a good steam-raiser in the tender engines. The only thing in common with the other Atlantic tanks was the use of the condensing gear, although this was modified.

The first 'I3' was released to traffic as No 21 in October 1907 and, after running-in, was put to work alongside the 'H1' Atlantics on the crack London expresses. Happily, it proved entirely successful, before performing unsurprisingly in an almost identical fashion to the 'B4s'. A water capacity of just 2,110 gallons was not unduly restrictive (the 'B4' tenders carried only 3,000 gallons), but it showed a surprisingly large appetite for coal, at 43.2lb per mile greater than that of the 'B4s' and the much more powerful 'H1s' (examples of which had recorded 40.33lb and 40.2lb per mile respectively in tests). This was not part of Marsh's plan for economy in working!

Perhaps No 21's high coal consumption was the reason Marsh at last decided to give superheating a try. As will be recalled, he had seen the Schmidt superheater in use in Germany whilst employed by the GNR and become something of a disciple. Basil Field was also a superheater enthusiast, and five superheated boilers were already on order from North British for the second part of the 'I2' construction programme, albeit delayed.

Five further superheater boilers, based on the 'B4' pattern, were ordered for the next batch of 'I3s', but due to production delays resulting from the reorganisation of the boiler shop an existing 'B4' boiler taken from No 47 was fitted with the Schmidt superheater intended for the second 'I3'. This boiler was pressed to 140lb/sq in, the figure for the saturated boiler on No 21 being 180lb/sq in. The superheated one was later raised to 160lb/sq in, the pressure for subsequent superheated boilers, and this was eventually raised to 180lb/sq in for all boilers, to match the saturated boilers' pressure.

The 'I3' design was thus redesigned to incorporate a Schmidt superheater together with 21in cylinders and 10in piston valves above them. Other alterations followed: the drivers were of 6ft 7½in diameter, and the wheelbase was extended between the rear bogie wheel and the front driven wheel by 3in to accommodate a longer smokebox for the superheater and the piston valves; the boiler had the standard 'B4' dimensions other than its heating surfaces and tube layout. The boiler, or, rather, the smokebox, was mounted on a separate saddle, and a heavy cast-iron dragplate was fitted below the cab to rebalance the weight, which was one ton greater than that of the slide-valve-fitted prototype, all of it carried on the front bogie wheels. The front bogie was no longer of the Billinton pattern but was based on the Doncaster swing-link design, which was giving successful service with the 'H1' tender engines. This locomotive, No 22, was released to traffic in May 1908 after problems with the cylinders and piston valves following completion (in March) had been overcome. Caution was the watchword on the Brighton, and the Board insisted that comparative trials between equal numbers of superheater-fitted and saturated-steam locomotives should be undertaken before any further orders be placed. No doubt they were very much aware that there was a royalty fee payable to Schmidt of £50 per superheater!

No 22 was a complete success and would make Marsh something of a celebrity in railway circles. Whether that was justified might warrant further analysis, but Basil Field's work was done under Marsh, and to the chief went all the credit. The 'I3s' would become known as the 'Wonder Engines', being capable of just about any task they were called upon to perform.

The first two 'I3s' were allocated to Brighton and New Cross respectively when new but in the autumn of 1908 were transferred to Battersea, where they were to be put through a series of stringent tests as required by the Board. During the course of these tests the first four of the five new superheated boilers were finally finished, so Nos 23-6 were built as superheated machines, being completed and released to traffic in February and March 1909. They (inevitably!) differed from No 22 through having 3in-longer frames to allow the piston valve rods to be removed more easily; No 22 had to have two large holes in the buffer-beam to achieve this. Nos 27-30 and 75/6 were then built using six new saturated boilers and released

to traffic in May 1909 (No 27), December 1909 (28/9) and March 1910 (30, 75/6), the slowness of their construction resulting from yet another period of unrest amongst the workforce at Brighton and Marsh's advice to the Board temporarily to suspend construction of new locomotives during late 1909. These saturated locomotives differed yet again from their predecessors in having 19in cylinders and ordinary piston valves rather than the slide valves of the saturated prototype, No 21.

Thus it was not until March 1910 that there were six 'I3s' of each kind available for comparative testing, and by this time it was obvious that the superheated locomotives were infinitely better machines. No 76 would be the last saturated main-line steam locomotive built for the Brighton. When compiling his definitive RCTS histories of Brighton locomotives Bradley had access to Works records that have since vanished, so his details, published in full in Volume 3 of that series constitute the only surviving record of the tests. To summarise, the saturated locomotives averaged 36.1lb per train mile, whilst the superheated engines achieved 30.5. The difference is less marked if lighting-up and awaiting-train times are included, the saturated machines using 39.4lb per mile overall and the superheated examples 34.2lb, but both figures are lower than those returned by the Atlantics and 'B4s' that were trialled at the same time.

As a result of the trials another batch of 'I3s' (which had been authorised but delayed pending the outcome of the trials), comprising five locomotives, was built with superheaters and released to traffic between October and December 1910. These were numbered 77-81, the last one being placed in service a matter of days before the first (and, as things turned out, only) example of Marsh's replacement design, 'J1' 4-6-2T No 325 *Abergavenny*, to which we shall return in the next chapter, as it has more bearing on the gestation and construction of the second batch of Atlantic tender engines. The last 'I3' of 1910 was to be the last Brighton locomotive to incorporate the ampersand in the company initials displayed on tank or tender sides. At the close of 1910 the 17 'I3s' built thus far were allocated to Brighton (Nos 25-8, 30, 75/7, 80/1), Battersea (21-4, 78), New Cross

(29, 79), Eastbourne (88) and St Leonards (76). It will be noted that saturated and superheated locomotives were freely mixed in these allocations, no particular distinction being drawn between the two types.

The long production cycle of the 'I3s' would extend well beyond Marsh's railway career, for his successor, Lawson Billinton, had yet another batch of 10 'I3s' (Nos 82-91) built between August 1912 and March 1913. This was either a testament to the brilliance of the 'I3s' or further evidence of the chaotic state of locomotive affairs on the railway. The locomotives themselves differed from their forebears only in the positioning of the front footplate steps and through being equipped with both the usual Westinghouse air brake

system and the vacuum system to enable them to work 'foreign' stock from other railways, which latter would prove very useful in the forthcoming war. But before concluding this chapter on the 'I3s' it is worth recording an interesting – and celebrated – episode in their history.

In their early days, when the saturated-steam-versus-superheated-steam trials were still underway, the superheated 'I3s' became involved, almost accidentally, in some rather different trials which were to raise Marsh's profile amongst Britain's locomotive engineers and establish superheating as the way forward in locomotive design.

Among the new services introduced in the summer of 1905 was a through train

ABOVE The second 'I3' was even more revolutionary although at the same time evolutionary, looking very similar to No 21 but boasting both a superheater and piston valves, the items which would prove to be the real legacy of these machines. Here No 22 is seen in the classic location on the Quarry line with a southbound 'Sunny South Express' in 1909, displaying four different varieties of Brighton headcode disc, although a square disc is something of a paradox! The chimney differs from that of the prototype, being somewhat straighter, while two small black dots on the buffer-beam below the number are the holes required to extract the piston valves.
Noodle Books

ABOVE The first of four views depicting members of the '13' class. No 22 is seen in an official company photograph, showing its short-lived bogie brakes and the smokebox saddle introduced to support the much heavier superheater-equipped boiler. The balancing dragweight at the cab end is not visible. Ian Allan Library

BELOW Comparing No 30 with No 22 reveals that there was little evidence externally that the latter was a saturated locomotive, aside from the pipework along the boiler and smokebox sides and the fact that it has just one set of guard-irons; No 22 had small irons on the bogie and larger items bolted to the buffer-beam. Ian Allan Library

ABOVE No 24 looks virtually identical to No 22, the only obvious difference being the holes in the latter's buffer-beam, which resulted in the production locomotives being 3in longer. *Ian Allan Library*

BELOW No 25 at Battersea shows the other side of the '13s' and the final Brighton livery for these locomotives. Its sanding gear has been simplified to feed abrasive grit to only the leading driving wheel in each direction. *Ian Allan Library*

LEFT AND BELOW Three photographs showing the opposite side of No 25 in its first livery (with ampersand) working a very short Brighton 'fast', No 79 of the post-Marsh final series and No 86 of the same series, emphasising the elegance of the design. These later locomotives were never fitted with bogie brakes and, despite being superheated from new, did not have the pipework associated with this fitting on the initial superheated series; they also had the simplified sanding gear from new.
Madgwick Collection (1), Ian Allan Library (2)

worked in association with the self-styled 'Premier Line', otherwise known as the London & North Western Railway. This train ran from Brighton via the West London line to Willesden and then via the West Coast main line through Rugby to Liverpool and Manchester. It was given the name 'Sunny South Special' and then 'Sunny South Express' when it was upgraded to a daily all-year-round service in 1906.

From their inception the 'I3s' worked alongside the 'H1s', taking even the heavy Pullman services in their stride, despite the apparent anomaly of being tank engines with only some 60% of the water capacity of the tender engines. This would be put to the test on the through train to/from the North West.

In the autumn of 1908 the first two 'I3s' had been transferred to Battersea, which shed provided power for the 'Sunny South Express'. Locomotives were changed at Willesden Junction, which made the run only a fraction longer for the locomotives than normal Brighton to Victoria or London Bridge trains. Battersea also received the first two production 'I3s', completed in February 1909, and during that year the effect of the superheaters upon their performance and economy became well known in railway circles.

Superheaters had been introduced to Great Britain by John Aspinall, of the Lancashire & Yorkshire Railway, who fitted them to some of his 'Highflyer' Atlantics. These were more or less 'steam dryers', a term used by Dugald Drummond of the LSWR to describe his early attempts at raising the temperature of steam.

On the GWR Churchward fitted a Schmidt superheater to one of his standard boilers but used it to develop his own 'Swindon' type, which was a cross between the steam-dryer type and the Schmidt, with a relatively low degree of superheating.

Churchward kept his developments close to his chest, so Marsh's experiments with the high degree of superheat offered by the Schmidt variety attracted a great deal of interest, notably on the LNWR. Accordingly the Brighton was approached by the latter with a request to run locomotives through to Rugby rather than change them at Willesden. This was agreed and, commencing in November 1909 for a total of 12 return journeys, the 'Sunny South Express' would live up to its name by running non-stop over the 77¼ miles from Willesden to Rugby without taking water between East Croydon and Rugby, a distance of 90½ miles. The round trip to or from Brighton would see locomotives working a total of 264 miles on alternate days, turn and turn about with the LNWR's offering.

The first 'production' 'I3', No 23, was chosen for the task, No 26 being held in reserve. Both were specially shopped at Brighton in October 1909 with the assistance of Schmidt's engineers, for the latter company

would benefit greatly if the tests went as anticipated. They did. Crewe provided one of George Whale's latest 'Precursor' 4-4-0s, No 7 *Titan*, and the North Western engineers had grave doubts as to whether the Brighton tank engine could compete over those mileages. Marsh must also have had some qualms, as emergency supplies of water were carried in the first luggage compartment of the train, which on occasions consisted of up to nine coaches plus a dining car, although the normal load was six coaches and the diner, weighing around 234 tons.

The churns proved unnecessary, as No 23 completed its allotted duties in exemplary fashion, returning to Brighton metals with ample water still in the tanks, coal in the bunker (this having been topped up at Rugby from bagged coal brought on the train) and on time. Overall, with No 26 only making one run, the 'I3s' averaged 22.4 gallons of water per mile and burned 27.4lb of coal per mile. *Titan* looked extravagant in comparison, using 36.6 gallons of water and 41.2lb of coal – 63% and 50% respectively *more* than the 'I3s'! It also often arrived at Brighton with a glowing smokebox door.

The direct result of the trials was that examples of the LNWR's new 'George the

Fifth' class (a development of the 'Precursor') then being built at Crewe were fitted with Schmidt superheaters and became the principal express locomotives on that railway in the last years before the Great War. But, despite this triumph, the atmosphere back at Brighton Works was becoming equally superheated, and it was Marsh who would get burned.

The Edwardian era came to an end on 6 May 1910, at a time of increasing chaos in locomotive affairs on the Brighton. Once again the backlog of repairs at Brighton Works was approaching crisis proportions, while construction of new locomotives had all but dried up, 1909 seeing production virtually halve to eight engines, the final 'I4' and seven 'I3s'. Just eight more 'I3s' plus the single 'J1' would appear in 1910 itself.

And then Marsh left the Brighton. His departure was somewhat traumatic, involving the 'H1' Atlantics and a 'ghost'.

THE MOST BEAUTIFUL ATLANTICS – THE 'H2s'

ABOVE The *real* No 36, *Abergavenny*, albeit numbered 325 upon completion, played a real part in the Brighton Atlantic story, over and above the resumption of naming certain express locomotives under Billinton Junior's spell in charge of LBSCR motive-power affairs. As built it looked very much like an elongated 'I3', the most notable difference being its outside cylinders and inside motion with 10in piston valves, this arrangement being adopted in its entirety for the second tranche of 'H'-class locomotives. The big tank is seen at **East Norwood** on an up fast train. Madgwick Collection

Beauty, it is said, is in the eye of the beholder, and there can be few enthusiasts who have not felt regret that none of the Brighton Atlantics has survived to this day, in particular none of those which 'completed the set' and brought the story full circle, these being the final six tender engines, classified 'H2'.

The locomotives in question, Nos 421-6, were ordered by Marsh's successor, Lawson Billinton, the son of his predecessor. Perhaps the only flaw in the appearance of the original 'H1s' was the retention of the Ivatt Atlantics' swooping running plate, which never seemed to make up its mind as to which direction to take. Marsh had at least improved upon that layout by making the actual surface continuous (Ivatt having made a break ahead of the cylinders), but Billinton Junior cleaned it up completely and produced a graceful continuous run from the sweep up in front of the cylinders to the reverse swoop down alongside the rear splashers – a minor change, but one which made a significant difference and transformed the entire look of the locomotive and, in the opinion of this writer, at least, created the most beautiful of all British Atlantic designs.

The production of these locomotives, like that of their forebears, is bound up in the horrendously complex history of Brighton Works, so I shall take up the story thereof as the second decade of the 20th century dawned. The year 1910 would see the backlog of maintenance once again build up to around 150 locomotives – approximately 30% of the company's locomotive stock – at a time when new construction had slowed to a trickle and traffic density was increasing. Blame had to be apportioned, and, once again, it fell upon the company's Locomotive, Carriage & Wagon Superintendent, this, of course, being Marsh. He was well aware of the situation and recommended the suspension of new locomotive construction for a short time whilst the backlog was cleared. He also suggested that it was time to build a new works, at Lancing, rather than to attempt, yet again, to reorganise Brighton.

Into this seemingly never-ending story now comes the character of Marsh himself. It will be recalled that he had had difficult relationships with work colleagues in his pre-Brighton days, and upon his elevation to high office with the LBSCR he had once again

made enemies, this time amongst the staff at Brighton Works. This was at the time of the rise of the trades-union movement, and he was ill-equipped to deal with organised labour, being somewhat autocratic in the old Victorian tradition. A strike had been only narrowly averted in 1909, and certain appointments amongst the staff, intended by Marsh to reduce costs for the ever-impoverished company, had backfired and caused further unrest. It was this, combined with the ongoing efforts to streamline and reorganise the Works, that led to the acute locomotive shortage.

As often happens in situations such as this, there were rumours circulating which

BELOW One of many official photographs of the first post-Marsh Brighton Atlantic, No 421, of the series ordered and 'tidied up' by Lawson Billinton, posed for the camera at Eastbourne. These locomotives were fitted from new with Hasler speed-recorders, although these would be removed before the Grouping, No 421 being the last to lose its 'spy in the cab', in September 1922. Noodle Books

seemingly suggested that Marsh was not a person of the utmost integrity – indeed, very much the opposite. One particular story concerned a rumoured sixth Atlantic, often referred to as the 'Ghost Atlantic'. If a story appears to have a basis in fact or can be made to look that way by the presentation of undisputed facts, it will gain credence. That of the Ghost Atlantic was one such and arose from a gap in the number series of new locomotives.

Like many pre-Grouping railway companies the Brighton had embarked upon a replacement programme for locomotives, frequently reusing the numbers of withdrawn locomotives for their replacements. The 'H1' Atlantics had received the numbers 37-41, and the various Atlantic tanks had been numbered upwards from 1 to 35. It was said that the Ghost Atlantic was to have been numbered 36, having been ordered at the same time as the other five 'H1s', and that Kitson had not erected it despite the fact that its parts, including the boiler, had been fabricated and delivered. Meanwhile Marsh, since taking up his appointment with the LBSCR in 1905, had moved to a house in Hove and had met the woman who shortly thereafter was to become his wife. She was from a relatively wealthy family, and the couple had acquired a laundry

business in Hove, which gave rise to a story that the boiler intended for the mythical No 36 had been delivered but diverted to Marsh's new laundry – at the expense of the railway! In the fetid atmosphere many people began to believe this seemingly incredible tale, and Marsh's authority was seriously undermined.

Within a few years construction work had actually begun on a new No 36, this being the number allocated initially to the first example of a brand-new Marsh design; an expansion of the successful 'I3' class, this large tank engine was at first designated 'I5' and later 'J1', being of a Pacific (4-6-2) layout. In line with established practice, parts for this machine were stamped with its proposed running number, so there were plenty of parts for an unbuilt No 36 to be seen within the works to lend credence to the story of the Ghost Atlantic.

Six 'J1s' were ordered, but only the first one was laid down, the intention being to gain experience before erecting the rest of the class. Renumbered 100 and then 325 before completion in December 1910 (so the rumourmongers saw parts for a No 36 but a No 100 or 325 being built) it was released to traffic with the name *Abergavenny* at the insistence of the Brighton Board, being the

ABOVE No 421 ran in Works grey for some time, from June 1911 until June 1913. When built it had a short cab roof, but this had been extended even before this photograph recorded its 'new' condition. Ian Allan Library

only Marsh locomotive to be named during his tenure. It proved to be powerful and reasonably economical, although, being substantially larger, it used 12-13% more water than did the 'I3s'.

Besides the vast increase in size, No 325's principal development lay in the design and location of its cylinders and valves. The latter were 10in piston valves located between the frames, whilst the cylinders, bored to 21in and with a 26in stroke, were outside the frames. Aside from enlargement to 22in by 28in for the later Baltic tanks (Billinton's enlargement of the 'J' tank design), this would remain the standard cylinder design for all subsequent Brighton steam-locomotive designs.

The year 1910 saw the production of just eight 'I3s' plus the solitary 'J1', but 1911 would see no more locomotives even started until May (when construction work began on the second 'J' tank, No 326), as a direct result of the dramas surrounding Marsh's career. Weighed down by

ABOVE AND BELOW The new Atlantics immediately became the 'top-link' Brighton locomotives, the solitary 'J1' being still officially on trial. The latter's sibling, 'J2' No 326 *Bessborough*, was completed by Billinton with outside Walschaerts valve gear, but no further locomotives were built until the first Baltic appeared, and these three locomotives were effectively all experimental 'one-offs'. The 11 Atlantics undertook all the regular express work, supplemented by the three big tanks plus the 'I3s', of which a further batch of 10 were ordered by Billinton after the 'H2s' entered service. These two photographs depict the second and fourth 'H2s', the latter destined to be the last Atlantic tender engine in BR service. Noodle Books, Ian Allan Library

ABOVE No 422 is seen again, this time at Merstham, a favourite viewpoint among contemporary photographers, who performed miracles with their heavy cameras. From this low angle the sky is bleached out, but the slow emulsions of the time were being rapidly sped up, so there are proportionately more photographs of moving trains from this era.
Madgwick Collection

the allegations, which became the subject of much speculation and investigation by the national press, Marsh, in February 1911, had applied for – and been granted – leave of absence on medical grounds. He duly retreated to Switzerland, Lawson Billinton being given authority to run the Locomotive Department during his absence.

We first heard about Lawson Billinton in Chapter 4, riding alongside Marsh on the footplate of 'I1' No 600 on the occasion of The Derby in June 1907. No doubt that *débâcle* imbued him with a healthy scepticism with regard to Marsh's design capabilities, and this must surely have been reinforced during his time as Assistant and, later, District Locomotive Superintendent at New Cross, where he was still in charge until transferred to Brighton Works to cover for Marsh's absence. In particular he would have been aware of the day-to-day failures of the small

Atlantic tanks of Classes I1 and I2 (10 of which worked from New Cross), the shortcomings of which were never properly resolved.

The press attention did the LBSCR no favours, especially in terms of the focus on the dreadful labour relations at Brighton Works and revelations of its backlog of repairs. Billinton, acting in Marsh's place but adopting a less confrontational approach, was able to placate the staff and reorganise affairs to the extent that, by the time Marsh finally tendered his resignation, on 11 July 1911, the backlog had been substantially reduced. Supportive as ever, the Brighton's Board of Directors rewarded Billinton by trying to entice Robert Urie from the LSWR to take over as Locomotive Superintendent! (The post of Locomotive, Carriage & Wagon Superintendent was split into its component parts at this time.) Urie refused to move, so, obviously reluctantly, the Board offered

Billinton the post with effect from 1 January 1912, although he was already effectively acting in that capacity – and would continue to do so for the remainder of 1911. No doubt this was another cost-cutting measure by the Board, as Billinton was offered the same salary – £1,500 per annum – that had been paid to Marsh some seven years earlier!

Faced with difficulties similar to those that had confronted Marsh upon his appointment –

in particular the urgent need for more express locomotives – and, due his own cynicism about Marsh's design capabilities, doubtful as to the merits of the as yet unproven Pacific tank, Billinton followed the same course adopted by Marsh in 1905 and recommended that requirements could be met only by the construction of a proven design. Thus was ordered, once again, a series of Atlantics that were outside the main stream of Brighton locomotive development. This time, however, thanks to Billinton's efforts, there was capacity to build the locomotives at Brighton Works, so

BELOW The elegant No 423 departs Victoria with a fast train for Brighton. The locomotives appeared thoroughly up to date at this time, but the stock they headed looked like a throwback to the Victorian Age, which it undoubtedly was. Only the occupants of the Pullman car, third in this formation, enjoyed a modicum of luxury. Electrification was absorbing a huge proportion of the Brighton company's capital, and there was no budget for modern express passenger stock. Noodle Books

the six Class 'H2s' were constructed there. The order was placed on 4 April 1911, authorisation having been given at the April meeting of the Locomotive Committee, so, technically, these Atlantics were ordered (and the first two delivered) during Marsh's term of office. Amazingly – and this is in no small part an endorsement of Billinton's organisational skills – the first, No 421, emerged from the Works just over two months later, in June 1911. This must be some sort of record for a new build, as the 'H2s' were not exact copies of the 'H1s', featuring as they did some significant mechanical alterations to the design in addition to the cosmetic alteration to the running boards. To get them built in such a short time Billinton had been authorised to pay for unlimited overtime by the Works staff in order to clear the maintenance backlog, which must have gone down very well! (Interestingly, Klaus Marx records that some work on drawings for superheated Atlantics had been done under Marsh's guidance by Basil Field and his team between February 1910 and March 1911, so Billinton's recommendation may well have been influenced by that and the locomotives may

have been actually ordered – and even started – some time before he recommended them!)

As always on the Brighton, it seems, the new Atlantics started life with one class designation which was swiftly altered, having been ordered as Class H1/s – the 's' standing for 'superheated'. This reflected the principal alteration to the design, the revised internal layout of the boiler dictating a change from slide valves to piston valves. These latter were already in use on the prototype 'J1', so the complete cylinder and piston-valve layout and motion was copied for the new Atlantics. Other changes to the 'H1' design included a reduction in boiler pressure to 170lb/sq in (from 200lb), an increase in the size of the cylinders to 21in x 26in (from 18½in or 19in x 26in) and the use 10in piston valves (in lieu of slide valves with Richardson strips), while the smokebox was now carried on a separate saddle. Cosmetic alterations in addition to the modified running plate included revised safety-valve casings and the chimney, the latter being a built-up parallel design.

Of all the alterations the reduction in the boiler pressure, often a side-effect of

BELOW The last 'new' design of British Atlantic was Vincent Raven's 'Z' class for the North Eastern Railway, of which the first 20 were built in 1911 (as were the Brighton 'H2s'), No 709 appearing at the end of July. The NER machines had three cylinders, and 10 were built superheated, the other 10 being saturated; the Brighton 'I3' lesson was still being learned! By 1918 a total of 50 had been built, all of which would be designated Class C7 by the LNER. The design was, in effect, 'stretched' to produce Raven's Class A2 Pacifics, which had no NER class code. The notion of stretching the Brighton Atlantics to produce Pacifics might be mind-boggling, but that is in effect what Gresley did during the Great War when drawing up his initial plans for a Pacific, his first proposal being a stretched Ivatt Atlantic. Ian Allan Library

superheating, would be the most significant, the 'H1s' having proven more fleet of foot than their Great Northern progenitors, and the same would be said of them in comparison with their offspring, the 'H2s'. Nevertheless, the 'H2s' were a Godsend to the Locomotive Department, and all had been delivered by the end of January 1912. As on the 'H1s', a short cab-roof was fitted, but this was extended before the first locomotive had its official photographs taken. Initial allocations were to Brighton (Nos 421/5), Battersea (422/6) and Eastbourne (423/4).

Once again it is necessary to remind ourselves of where the new Atlantics fitted in within the general run of British steam power. Just one Pacific tender engine had been built, in 1908, this being Churchward's 'Super Star' No 111 *The Great Bear* on the Great Western Railway. Viewed as something of a monstrosity even by its designer, who had had it built as a sop to his Board of

Directors (who wanted a 'super-sized' locomotive), it remained a singleton and was eventually rebuilt as a 'Castle' 4-6-0, this class being the true enlargement of the 'Star' design. In 1911 the four-cylinder 'Stars' represented the apogee of British steam-locomotive design, and Churchward, after building the first of these and a number of the two-cylinder 'Saints' as Atlantics, had already converted them to 4-6-0s (which layout was adopted for all further express locomotives). The LNWR had, after learning the lesson of superheating from the 'I3s', started building 4-6-0s in great numbers, but no new Atlantic designs would appear after the 'H2s' other than Vincent Raven's 'Z' class on the NER. The Great War would delay the introduction of more powerful express steam locomotive designs for some years.

The Brighton crews took to the new 'H2s' as quickly as they had the earlier 'H1s', and these locomotives settled down to become the

railway's principal express locomotives. Strangely, whilst they were used on trains to Eastbourne and Newhaven, they were not used regularly on the company's longer lines through West Sussex to Bognor, Littlehampton and Portsmouth, such services generally remaining in the hands of the 'B4s' and, latterly, the 'I3' tanks, as well as the veteran 'Gladstones'.

Despite the success of the 'H2s', when the time came in 1912 for some more express locomotives to be built Billinton reverted to the construction of a further batch of 10 Class 'I3' tank engines (Nos 82-91), notwithstanding the progress made with the two 'J'-class Pacific tanks and his own work which in 1914 would produce the first of the 'L'-class Baltics (of which more anon). The Brighton was a strange railway, at least in locomotive matters! It would appear that they had been authorised and ordered during Marsh's tenure but not built. This is rather at odds with Billinton's plan to build the Atlantics as an 'emergency' order, since 'I3' production was already set up, if somewhat erratic. No one has put forward any argument as to why this course of events was followed, and I too have been unable to uncover any reasons.

Although in this book we are concerned with the Atlantics, for the sake of completeness – and in order to place them in the context of the Brighton company's convoluted locomotive history in the 20th century – it should be noted that Billinton completed a second 'J'-class locomotive, numbered 326. The only change he made was to substitute Walschaerts valve gear for the Stephensons used on No 325, the alteration being sufficient to warrant a revised classification, 'J2'. Rather than fulfil the balance of the order for 'J'-class engines he then went on to enlarge the design still further to produce the Class 'L' 4-6-4 (Baltic) tanks, with a greatly increased water capacity. This would bring its own problems, the locomotives suffering a number of accidents caused by the effects on running associated with large quantities of water surging within the side tanks. Such problems would recur more than once in the British pursuit of the use of large tank engines on express work. The 'I3s' and the two 'Js' probably proved to be the most satisfactory such designs, although the results of using large express tanks would have a later bearing on the history of the Brighton Atlantics.

ABOVE Two for the price of one. Bearing Billinton's large numerals, 'H2s' Nos 421 and 425 stand under the roof at Victoria. Just visible on the right is 'H1' No 39 *La France*. Ian Allan Library/O. J. Morris/D. J. W. Brough collection

CHAPTER 7

PRIDE OF THE BRIGHTON

ABOVE The final Marsh-era locomotives were the 10 additional 'I3s' ordered by Billinton in 1911, No 82 being the first of this batch, released to traffic in August 1912. Allocated to New Cross shed from new, it is seen on an Arun Valley train at Arundel. This batch lacked cab-roof clerestories and ventilators, as the tanks inside the cabs were cooler as a result of improved insulation and the re-routeing of the steam exhaust pipes upwards and rearwards along the cab roofs to help prevent the lookout windows from becoming misted over. In addition the buffer-beam ends were cut away to improve clearances.
Madgwick Collection

The Brighton's collection of Atlantic locomotives was completed in March 1913 with the delivery of No 91, the last of the Marsh-designed, Billinton-built final batch of 'I3s'. Pride of the fleet, of course, were the tender engines, although the 'H1s' were not outshone by their younger 'H2' siblings; as previously noted, they were considered more speedy (this being usually ascribed to their higher boiler pressure) and remained at the top of the Brighton roster. No 39 continued to hog the limelight, being used for a couple of prestigious workings in 1911 and 1913. The first of these occasions arose on 24 June 1911, when it was chosen to take the new king, George V, to Portsmouth for the Coronation Fleet Review at Portsmouth. Two years later it became the first of the Marsh Atlantics to bear a name, being specially prepared to head a train, also to Portsmouth, conveying the French President, Raymond Poincaré, and was named *La France* for the occasion. The name was painted in the same style as those borne by the 'B4s', hand-painted on the splashers, although in this case on the rear splashers rather than the front. Shortly thereafter the country after it which was named, along with Great Britain itself, became embroiled in war with Germany, which effectively stifled progress on the Brighton.

Upon the outbreak of war the 73 Brighton Atlantics were spread throughout the company's network, being allocated as follows:

Class H1	Brighton:	37-41

Class H2	Brighton:	421/5
	Battersea:	422/6
	Eastbourne:	423/4

Class I1	Brighton:	6, 595/7-9
	Battersea:	2-5, 7, 8
	New Cross:	9, 10, 600-4
	Tunbridge Wells:	1, 596

Class I2	Brighton:	12
	Battersea:	15/6
	Eastbourne:	14/9
	Horsham:	13, 20
	New Cross:	17/8
	Tunbridge Wells:	11

Class I3	Brighton:	25-8, 30, 75/7, 80/1/3/5/9, 91
	Battersea:	21-4, 78, 87
	Eastbourne:	88
	New Cross:	29, 79, 82/4/6, 90
	St Leonards:	76

Class I4	Brighton:	35
	Battersea:	31/2/3/4

At this time no significant changes had been made to any of the locomotives, although the provision of new boilers for six of the 'I1' class made a marginal improvement to their steaming. These were Nos 3 (October 1913), 602 (November 1913), 598 (August 1915), 596 (September 1915), 7 (March 1916) and 600 (May 1920). The class remained on light

BELOW Another view of one of the later Marsh Atlantics, No 422, again with the Billinton numbers and 'L B S C' (without ampersand) on the tender. The splendid finish on these locomotives would soon be compromised by the exigencies of wartime. *Madgwick Collection*

LEFT AND ABOVE Efforts to avoid war included the visit of the French President, Raymond Poincaré, in the summer of 1913, for which occasion 'H1' Atlantic No 39 was named *La France* and elaborately decorated, perhaps to reassure the French that their traditional enemy was now their friend, as British diplomacy concentrated on preventing Germany's empire from expanding.
Madgwick Collection, Ian Allan Library

duties throughout the war and remained so employed following the Grouping.

Such was the esteem in which the 'I2s' and 'I4s' were (not) held that during the war they were frequently used for the least demanding duty of all – effectively as mobile carriage-warmers, No 19 performing this duty at Eastbourne and Nos 11/5/6 likewise at Victoria. No 13 warmed Brighton Works. No 35 was loaned to the Longmoor Military Railway for seven weeks in 1915 and again during the summer of 1916. Its appearance changed slightly following damage inflicted by an LNWR goods engine at Three Bridges, for when repaired at Brighton it had the

corners of its buffer-beam cut away like the 'I3s'; Bradley speculates that it was probably mistaken for one of the latter, as the smaller tanks did not experience the problems with clearances that were encountered by the 'I3s'. It seems unlikely that any of the footplate crews would have made that mistake!

The modification of 'I3' buffer-beams continued throughout the war years, but the most significant change to any of this successful class was the conversion in 1919 of the initial, saturated-steam locomotive (No 21) to superheat. Although new cylinders were supplied the slide valves were retained – an unusual situation, as piston valves were

usually *de rigueur* for superheated designs at the time. Its appearance was altered due to the extended smokebox, but no smokebox saddle was fitted, so the locomotive maintained a unique appearance. Although Lawson Billinton recommended the superheating of the saturated 'I3s' (and the 'H1s') in 1920, they would not be so converted until after the Grouping; indeed one new saturated boiler had been provided as late as 1916, to create a spare. Superheated No 76 joined its youngest siblings by becoming dual-fitted with the addition of vacuum-brake equipment in June 1918.

Throughout the Brighton's final years the tender engines remained much as built, although the 'H1s' received 'H2'-style chimneys between March 1914 and November 1919; most also lost their Doncaster safety-valve casings in favour of the Field-designed flared replacements at the same time, the exception being No 37, which retained its original safety-valve casing into Southern days, finally losing this feature in August 1924.

LEFT No 39 at Brighton Works with a classmate, possibly a month or two before its naming. The original caption for this photograph records the pair as 'under construction' at Brighton, but as they were the products of Kitsons in Leeds this must be an overhaul. In the foreground is Stroudley 'Gladstone' No 189 *Edward Blount*, withdrawn in December 1912 and perhaps in the process of being dismantled.
Madgwick Collection/M. P. Bennett/Bluebell Archives

ABOVE The penultimate '13', seen in absolutely superb condition. Rows of holes just under the lip of the cab roof provide ventilation in the absence of a clerestory and ventilators, whilst the exhaust pipe from the tank top to the roof is clearly visible. The 10 locomotives of this batch were fitted with both the normal Westinghouse air brakes and a vacuum ejector to enable them to work trains from other companies; they were also equipped with Bosch auto-lubricators. *Madgwick Collection*

BELOW The first Atlantic, No 37, pictured ready to leave Brighton during the war. Its appearance now shows how the reduction in the cheap labour force, as active men were called up, has led to a deterioration in the once spotless condition of its paintwork. Unlike World War 2, the Great War saw little damage inflicted on Britain's railways, but the maintenance backlog at the cessation of hostilities left them in a poor state, such that consideration was given to nationalisation. *Madgwick Collection*

ABOVE At the end of the war standards of cleanliness were regained, albeit slowly. No 39 remained the only named Atlantic right through to the Grouping of the railways, this being the compromise whereby nationalisation was avoided. No 39's final coat of umber would weather so well that it was retained until January 1926. No 38's lasted nearly as long, until December 1925, by which time this locomotive had been named *Portland Bill* (since May of that year), so in fact two Atlantics bore names whilst wearing Brighton livery.
Madgwick Collection (both)

Hasler speed-recorders (fitted to all the 'H2s' from new) had appeared on 'H1s' Nos 39-41 in 1909. These were also fitted 'I3s' Nos 22 and 80, although the former gave up its equipment to No 81, which in turn passed it on to Baltic tank No 329. Baltics also received speed-recorders from Nos 425/6, but the remaining four 'H2s' retained theirs until 1922. Both 'H1' and 'H2' classes had been built with bogie brakes, but these were removed during Brighton days.

Duties for all the Atlantics barely changed in the years leading up to the Grouping, as the only additions to the express passenger stock were the Billinton Class L Baltics; two of these were built in 1914, the other five emerging only in the Brighton's final years, between October 1921 and April 1922. Thus in 1920 there were only 11 'H'-class Atlantics, 27 'I3s', two 'Js' and two 'Ls' for express work,

the 33 'B4' 4-4-0s providing a secondary function on semi-fast and cross-country services. One of the latter had recently been rebuilt with a superheater as Class B4X, but the superheating programme had stalled, and only one more would be rebuilt before 1923. Also providing power for secondary services were the 25 'B2X' 4-4-0s, the programme instigated by Marsh in 1907 to re-boiler them with 'C3' goods-engine-type boilers having been completed as recently in 1916. A number of the Stroudley Class B1 'Gladstone' were still in use on secondary trains, so all in all the Brighton was about to bequeath the Southern something of a motive-power problem. The spread of suburban electrification, meanwhile, had little effect on the smaller Atlantic tanks, which had long since been relegated to lighter duties and, indeed, would soon be slated for withdrawal.

ABOVE At the end of the Brighton's existence, on 31 December 1922, the 'I2s' and 'I4s' were still working on secondary duties, many of which involved commuter work to London. 'I2' No 12 is pictured c1922/3 at the head of a Tunbridge Wells West–London Bridge train emerging from Limpsfield Tunnel. *Madgwick Collection*

CHAPTER 8

MAUNSELL AND THE SOUTHERN

ABOVE AND FACING PAGE The early Southern period saw few changes to the Brighton Atlantic fleet, other than renumbering with the addition of the letter 'B' as a prefix to the original Brighton numbers. The principal change was to the paintwork, Billinton's hard-wearing umber livery slowly giving way to Maunsell's olive green. The first of the 'H2s', by now No B421, donned a coat of green in September 1924, and both sides of the locomotive are seen here, although the 'B' prefix is better seen on the side of 'I3' No 80. The two brake pipes standing proud of the buffer-beams on both locomotives are indicative of the fitting of vacuum ejectors to the remaining members of their respective classes following the Grouping, vacuum braking having been adopted as standard by the **Southern.** Madgwick Collection (1), Ian Allan Library (2)

Monday 1 January 1923 saw all 73 Brighton Atlantics taken into Southern Railway stock. The new company's Chief Mechanical Engineer was Richard Maunsell, latterly of the South Eastern & Chatham, who would continue that railway's policy regarding locomotive development, laced with modifications to that of the LSWR, which company's CME, Robert Urie, would retire from railway work almost immediately. Lawson Billinton remained in post for a further six months, until 30 June 1923, before retiring to become a fruit farmer. Thus ended Brighton influence in terms of locomotive design, although Maunsell's Class Z shunting tank would use a boiler derived from that of the Marsh 'C3' goods 0-6-0.

The Atlantics (the larger locomotives, at least) were performing satisfactorily, so there was no immediate need for change, aside from renumbering and repainting to reflect their new ownership. 'Renumbering' entailed the simple prefixing of existing identities with the letter 'B' to reflect the name of the works responsible for maintenance of the locomotive (ex-LSWR types being prefixed 'E', for Eastleigh, and ex-SECR 'A', for Ashford). The livery was changed from Marsh's smart umber (which had been perpetuated by Billinton) to

a dark green, known as olive green. Repainting was normally effected during general overhaul, so the process took time to complete, although most express locomotives would be dealt with during the first three years of Southern ownership. 'H2' No 422 was the first, emerging in green livery as No B422 in May 1924.

The 'I3s' were generally fast, consistent and effective machines, but the six 'production' saturated locomotives used more fuel than the saturated examples, and, following the

successful conversion of the prototype, No 21 (now B21), a priority task for Brighton Works under the new regime was to convert the remainder, No B28 becoming the first of these, in October 1923. The process was fairly drawn out, as the locomotives gave perfectly satisfactory service, the last, No B29, not being modified until September 1927. For some reason three different cylinder sizes were used in the conversions, Nos B28 and B76 receiving 19in bored cylinders like No B21, No B27 20in,

and Nos B30 and B75 21in. There seems to have been no discernible difference in their performance; at least, there is no record of such.

The Brighton's electrification of suburban lines was continued by the Southern Railway and resulted in many of the earlier Stroudley and Billinton tank engines' becoming surplus to requirements in the London area and thus available for use elsewhere. These were rather more useful than the smaller Atlantic tanks, which were coming up for major overhaul and were considered ready for scrapping by early 1925; the latter's boilers, it was felt, would be more usefully employed upgrading the better examples of the older classes. However, Brighton Works was engaged in an extensive programme of superheating the 'B4s', for which a number of new boilers of the 'K'-class type were ordered. This left surplus a pool of original 'B4' boilers , so the Works Manager suggested that these be used on the 'I1s' to avoid scrapping locomotives that had not yet achieved 20 years of service. Superheating, although considered, was not undertaken, but the larger fireboxes were thought to constitute a worthwhile upgrading to improve the steaming ability of these locomotives, which

would now more closely resemble smaller-wheeled versions of the 'I3s'.

Maunsell agreed with the plan, and in the spring of 1925 No B596 was admitted to works for rebuilding. This was quite extensive, the larger boiler (4ft 10in diameter instead of 4ft 3in) having to be pitched some 4in higher in the frames to lift the longer 'B4' firebox clear the axles of the coupled wheels; it thus required a smokebox saddle and the provision of a new cab based on that of Maunsell's 'River'-class 2-6-4 tank engine (10 of which were then under construction at Brighton). This cab was placed further back on the frames, as the 'new' boilers were considerably longer and the coal bunker was shortened to allow this resulting in a reduction of capacity by a quarter of a ton to 2¾ tons. A Maunsell smokebox door was fitted, giving the rebuilds a much more contemporary appearance. Curiously they retained the troublesome condensing apparatus, poor lubrication of the slide valves and Stroudley boiler feed-water equipment, all of which would have been changed had they been superheated at the same time.

The resultant locomotive was classified 'I1X', the 595-604 series, with their longer coupled wheelbase, being the first to be dealt with, emerging in rebuilt form between July 1925 and October 1927. The second-hand components used in the construction of Nos 1-10 caused a few problems and hence a delay in converting them, these locomotives emerging in rebuilt form between October 1929 and February 1932 (although most of their inherited parts, notably the wrought-iron wheel centres, had already been replaced, further emphasising the fallacy of the LBSCR Locomotive Committee's reasoning back in 1907). Rebuilding provided the Central Section (as the former Brighton lines became known under the Southern) with a class of useful secondary small tank engines, many of which were employed on services from Tunbridge Wells West, taking over duties from the later 'I2s' and 'I4s'.

The 'Rivers' mentioned above were Nos A800-9, being built for the Eastern Section (the former SECR lines), but 10 earlier 'Rivers' had been supplied to the Central Section in May and June 1925 as Nos A791-9. The prototype of this class, No A790, had been built by the SECR in June 1920 and was transferred to the Central Section in early 1925. This type of 2-6-4 tank was Maunsell's equivalent of the Brighton's Marsh 'J'-class Pacifics and subsequent Billinton Baltics and formed part of his range of standardised locomotive designs which also included the 2-6-0 tender engines of Classes N and (later) U. The 'Rivers' received their names as part of the Southern's drive to raise its public profile, the policy being extended to all of the company's express passenger locomotives.

Former Brighton locomotives falling into this category included the Baltics and, relevant to our story, the 'H1' and 'H2' Atlantics but not the 'I3s', which were the victims of downgrading as the 'Rivers' were introduced.

Naming of the 'H1s' and 'H2s' was a protracted affair, generally being effected as locomotives came in for overhaul and repainting in Southern livery. Full details and particulars of the type of nameplates employed will be found in Appendix II. They made no difference, of course, to the locomotives themselves but appeared to confirm that, although up to 20 years old (in the case of the 'H1s'), they were still considered top-link express locomotives. However, from 1926 a number of both classes were transferred to work fast services from Eastbourne and Bognor Regis, as the 'Rivers' (of which more anon), together with a series of 'King Arthurs', became the top-link engines on the Brighton main line.

The 'Rivers' feature again in our story owing to a series of accidents involving these locomotives on the Eastern Section during

1926 and 1927, culminating in the Sevenoaks disaster of 24 August 1927, in which the first Brighton-built example, No A800, left the rails at high speed, resulting in the loss of 13 lives and many injuries. The Southern immediately withdrew all of the locomotives, which meant that, as a stopgap, 'I3s' had to be reinstated on fast services.

A longer-term consequence of the accident was that the negative publicity prompted the company to reconsider the use of large tank engines on express trains. Maunsell must already have had reservations, for in 1925, while the 'Rivers' were still being delivered, he had ordered, for use on Brighton services, a batch of 14 'King Arthur' 4-6-0 tender engines, based on a Urie LSWR design. These had been delivered between March 1926 and January 1927 for the principal express services on the Central Section, on which, together with the 10 'Rivers', they effectively superseded ex-LBCSR locomotives. To fill the gap caused by the withdrawal of the 'Rivers' eight ex-LSWR Class L12 and six Class T9 4-4-0s were transferred to the Central Section.

This all took place at a time when the Southern was rapidly expanding its electrification, now using the LSWR system of third-rail power distribution, hitherto considered as suitable only for suburban systems, as opposed to the Brighton's overhead system, which was seen as more suited to main lines. In fact the Southern had decided to abolish the Brighton system and standardise on the third rail for all electrification, so some routes were electrified twice in five years; the final overhead project resulted in electric trains running as far south as Coulsdon North, on the main line to Brighton, from 1 April 1925, but by 23 September 1929 the wires had been replaced by the third rail. Between these dates the third rail was also extended to the other ex-LBSCR suburban lines.

The year 1929 was one of tremendous import for the erstwhile Brighton system and

thus for the Atlantics. In that year the SR's General Manager, Sir Herbert Walker, obtained authority from the Board to continue the process of electrifying the whole of the main line to Brighton together with the first part of the western coastal line as far as Worthing, effectively extending the Coulsdon scheme. The discredited 'Rivers' had been rebuilt as nameless 'U'-class 2-6-0 tender engines and redeployed elsewhere, so the existing express-locomotive fleet would now have to hold the fort on the main line until electric trains took over, this being scheduled for 1 January 1933 although electric services as far as Three Bridges would commence as early as 17 July 1931. Thus the 'H1s' and 'H2s' enjoyed something of an Indian summer on principal fast trains, while the 'I3s' were eased out or redeployed on the cross-country trains over the secondary main lines, bringing about the end for the famous 'Gladstones'.

Meanwhile the smaller Atlantics continued to be used on local services throughout the network. In common with all ex-LBSCR locomotives all of the Atlantics would soon have their numbers altered, this time by the addition of 2,000 to the existing number and deletion of the 'B' prefix.

Almost as soon as the main line was fully 'juiced' inroads were made into the Atlantics. This initially affected the well-nigh useless 'I2s', the oldest, No B11, going in January 1933 without being renumbered. It was quickly followed by Nos B14 and B19, and all had gone by Easter 1936 save Nos 2013/7/9, which were in use as carriage pilots at Brighton. Although it infringes upon the era described in the next chapter, it is probably as well dispose of these engines herein: the 'I4s' started to go at the beginning of 1936, and it was all over for these two classes by July 1937 with the exception of 'I2s' Nos 2013 and 2019 and 'I4' No 2034. The latter enjoyed another three years on work around Brighton and up to Tunbridge Wells West and Horsham, substituting for 'B4s', finally being withdrawn in May 1940.

The two late-surviving 'I2s' had an interesting final few years, finally being withdrawn in November 1937 (No 2019) and January 1939 (2013) but not broken up, due to the prospect of war. Initially they were used as an air-raid shelter at Bournemouth shed, but in March 1942 they were purchased by the War Department for use on the Longmoor

LEFT AND BELOW Two further 'I3s' illustrate some of the changes introduced following the Grouping. The SR had commenced equipping the saturated 'I3s' with superheating; No B27 is seen at Fratton with a train of ex-LSWR stock, whilst No B89 has charge of a set of ex-SECR 'Birdcage' six-wheel close-coupled suburban stock on the Brighton main line in 1924, under wires which were still being extended in early Southern days.
Madgwick Collection, Ian Allan Library

Military Railway, for which they were overhauled at Ashford. Numbered 2400/1 and later 72400/1, they remained in use until the end of the war and were withdrawn in October 1946. Moved to a siding near Guildford in 1949, they were broken up there two years later, so they could be said to have survived into BR days, albeit not ownership!

As for the 'H1s' and 'H2s', the Brighton main-line electrification of 1933 meant that they had to be redeployed elsewhere on the Southern system. At this time they were still allocated to Bognor Regis and Eastbourne sheds, the former having Nos 2423-6, Eastbourne the rest; Nos 2038/9 were soon transferred to Newhaven for the boat trains, while the other five Eastbourne engines went to London, to New Cross shed, from where they worked, *inter alia*, trains to Brighton via Uckfield, although they were barred from the services through East Grinstead via the Bluebell route.

The Brighton had always had a very generous loading gauge in comparison with the other Southern constituent companies, so the Atlantics had to be modified to conform

with the 'composite' SR loading gauge, which meant that tall items such as chimneys, domes and cab-roof ventilators needed to be reduced in height, and extremities such as the cab-roof shoulders and footsteps adjusted. The 'I1X' tank engines were already being rebuilt with this in mind, so it was the tender engines and the 'I3s' that required attention. (For the record, the Baltic tanks were subjected to more extreme measures, being rebuilt as 4-6-0 tender engines – and very unsatisfactory they were – whilst the two 'J' tanks were modified in much the same way as their 'I3' cousins.)

The modifications were applied first in mid-1935 to 'H1' No 2041 and 'I3' No 2084 and altered considerably the appearance of each. Most noticeable were the shorter chimney and the rounded cab contours, which made both locomotives look much more modern. There were variations between members of each class, some receiving flatter-topped domes, others not receiving cab alterations and still others being fitted with boilers sporting 'snifting valves' on the smokebox – an outward indication of a change of superheater from the original

FACING PAGE AND ABOVE The first change to affect the 'H1' and 'H12s' was the decision taken in 1925 to name them all – a process that took some considerable time. In addition the well-known *La France*, by now numbered B39, was renamed *Hartland Point* in January 1926, at the same time gaining SR olive-green livery. The two 'H2s' seen here also received their names upon repainting, No B426 becoming *St. Alban's Head* in June 1925, and No B425 *Trevose Head* more than a year later, in August 1926. Painted red, the nameplates lent something extra to these locomotives, which were still to be seen on the 'Southern Belle' despite the presence on the Central Section of seven Baltic tanks, 10 'Rivers' and 14 'King Arthurs'. *Madgwick Collection (1), Ian Allan Library (2)*

Schmidt type to one of Maunsell's own design, on which he had standardised for all superheated locomotives of the Southern. Most of the differences occurred within the 'I3' class: the first example to be dealt with, No 2084, had all the changes, including a new smooth-barrelled chimney to bring the height down to 12ft 11½in from its original 13ft 0⅞in. Some locomotives had to wait a considerable time to receive the revised chimney, whilst Nos 2021/2 and 2075-81 retained their clerestory roofs.

Perhaps the most significant change to affect the 'I3s' – albeit one that made no alteration to them physically – manifested itself on 1 February 1937 in the form of a list of new restrictions as to where they could work; included within the Eastern and Central Sections Engine Restriction Book, this banned them from the Three Bridges–Ashurst Junction, Horsted Keynes–Culver Junction and Redgate Mill–Polegate lines (despite the fact that the class was in the throes of being altered to *increase* its sphere of operation!) owing to the state of certain bridges in the area served by Tunbridge Wells West's locomotive allocation. Their duties on these lines were passed over to the 'I1X' class.

ABOVE The early 1930s saw an alteration to the numbering of the entire Southern fleet, whereby the clumsy prefix letters used hitherto were replaced by numerals, former LBSCR locomotives having 2,000 added to their original numbers. No 2426 *St. Alban's Head* looks particularly smart following an overhaul at Eastleigh Works, which had taken over responsibility for the Atlantics. A small change was the insetting of the footsteps on the locomotive, to provide the clearance necessary for use, if required, on the **Eastern Section.** Ian Allan Library

BELOW The first Brighton Atlantic (by now named *Selsey Bill*) became a superheated locomotive in March 1927, the only outward sign of this extremely significant alteration being a new smokebox saddle. Surprisingly the superheater was a Schmidt unit, as used on the 'H2s', although Maunsell was this time providing his own design of superheater for new locomotives and conversions of other types such as the ex-LSWR 'T9s'. Retaining their higher boiler pressure of 200lb/sq in (compared to the 170lb of the 'H2s'), the 'H1s' were now regarded as superior on the road. Ian Allan Library

ABOVE All five 'H1s', together with the first two 'H2s', were reallocated to Eastbourne when the Brighton main line was electrified on 1 January 1933. No 2421 *South Foreland* is seen here on the latter, with an express consisting of SR Maunsell stock plus a single Pullman car. Ian Allan Library

BELOW Electrification would soon affect the two later classes of small Atlantic tanks. Despite being slightly better than the 'I1s' the 'I2s' and 'I4s' were not rebuilt like the earlier class and were allowed to work out their days relatively unchanged. Still to be renumbered when photographed in 1933, 'I2' No B13 would be one of the final withdrawals and was destined for an afterlife. Ian Allan Library

ABOVE Seen at Eastleigh after withdrawal in July 1937, 'I4' No 2032 shows the final form of this superheated class, having been modified to meet the composite loading gauge, applicable from 1935; alterations included a shorter chimney, curved corners to the cab roof, re-siting of the whistle (to the safety-valve casing) and inset steps. It would remain at Eastleigh until cut up during the week ending 6 September 1940. Ian Allan Library

BELOW Like sister No 2013, 'I2' No 2019 was destined to lead an afterlife, initially as an air-raid shelter at Bournemouth and later as an Army locomotive on the Longmoor Military Railway, where from April 1942 both locomotives were used on passenger services between Bordon and Longmoor. Railway Correspondence & Travel Society

ABOVE AND BELOW Official portraits of 'H1' No 2041 and 'H2' No 2422 reveal the only major changes to these classes' appearance in their long lives, the results of being cut down so as not to exceed the SR's composite loading gauge. No 2041 was the first to be dealt with, in August 1935, the fitting of a Maunsell 'U1'-pattern chimney being the most obvious change. Other changes included a reduction of the dome, removal of the whistle from the cab roof (and replacement by an LSWR Drummond-pattern one on the safety-valve casing) and lowering of the safety-valve levers; the cab roof too was lowered and rounded off slightly, the steps were inset, and the coal rails on the tender were fitted with sheet-metal backing. On the 'H2' a Maunsell superheater at last made an appearance, evidenced by the snifting valves on either side of the smokebox behind the chimney, but although No 2041 had also gained one during its 'cutting-down' overhaul, for some reason it failed to receive the snifting valves. Both types also gained standard Southern lamp-irons. Ian Allan Library (both)

ABOVE AND RIGHT 'H1' No 2039 *Hartland Point* became the second of its class to receive a Maunsell superheater when altered in July 1935 to comply with the constraints of the composite loading gauge, and this was evidenced by the fitting of snifting valves, as seen in this view of the locomotive in charge of the 'Sunny South Express' at Purley on 16 August 1938. But for the snifting valves (which in any case were destined for a short life, as Bulleid would soon have them removed), *Beachy Head*, pictured that same month at Newhaven, having arrived with a boat train from Victoria, was now in the form in which it would later gain fame. Madgwick Collection, C. C. B. Herbert/Madgwick Collection

LEFT 'I1X' No 2007 is seen at the end of the Maunsell era at Tunbridge Wells West shed, where its lighter weight gave it new duties over lines from which the 'I3s' were banned from the beginning of February 1937. From this angle the formerly dainty and ineffectual 'I1' now looks like a very modern and effective machine!

Author's collection

ABOVE AND BELOW The '13s' also were cut-down to the composite loading gauge, but the most noticeable change, to lower chimneys, was not effected immediately. Here No 2090 has been cut down but still retains its original Basil Field chimney, whilst cut-down No 2075 additionally retains its clerestory cab roof as it takes water in 1936. Both locomotives have flat-topped domes.

Ian Allan Library, Madgwick Collection

CHAPTER 9

THE BULLEID ERA

ABOVE The last four 'H2s' were working on the Arun Valley line when Bulleid took over as CME of the Southern in 1937. No 2425 *Trevose Head* is seen in charge of the 3.20pm Victoria–Bognor Regis train at Hackbridge on 25 June 1938, a week before electrification would eliminate these duties altogether and place a question mark over the future of the 'H1'- and 'H2'-class Atlantics. This locomotive had had its boiler pressure boosted to 200lb/sq in in January 1938 so was now the equal of the older 'H1' locomotives.
Madgwick Collection

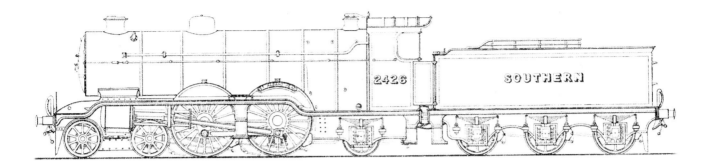

At the end of October 1937 Maunsell retired as CME, to be replaced by the mercurial Oliver Vaughan Snell Bulleid, hitherto Sir Nigel Gresley's principal assistant on the LNER. Gresley had himself been the chief assistant to Henry Ivatt on the GNR and had developed the Ivatt Atlantic design into his own celebrated Pacifics for that company and for the LNER. Thus when Bulleid arrived on the Southern he would have been familiar with the design of the 11 'H1' and 'H2' Atlantics, for these were, as we have seen, essentially Ivatt locomotives; indeed the final series of GNR examples had been superheated and fitted with piston valves in a manner very similar to the 'H2s'.

Further electrification was in progress at the time of Bulleid's appointment, and it was with the buffet cars for the Bognor services that he first made his mark, by painting them in what was, for its time, a very lurid green livery, which was to be the basis of his later malachite-green locomotive livery. The Atlantics had been redeployed within the Central Section from 1926, but following the Brighton electrification in 1933 (after which the Central Section 'King Arthurs' were transferred to the Eastern Section) and that to Eastbourne in 1935 (which had led to the rebuilding of the Baltics and their transfer to the Western Section) they had been left as the Central Section's principal express locomotives, frequently being moved to new pastures. These had included the Newhaven boat trains from 1933, Nos 2039 and 2424 being so employed at the outbreak of World War 2, although these ceased in May 1940, when the 'Phoney War' was brought to an end by the German invasion of Belgium and France. The final prewar electrification, to Portsmouth, had left the Atlantics with no main-line duties on the Central Section, so

Nos 2421/3/5/6 were lent to the Eastern Section for the summer of 1938. They were not needed the following year, as the Medway electrification was also inaugurated in that last peacetime summer, so the gradual decline in their fortunes might be said to have started at this time.

It is well known that Gresley had a soft spot for the Ivatt locomotives and had made many modifications to them, including the fitting of a booster engine to one. Bulleid would leave the Brighton examples well alone other than to increase the boiler pressure of the later series to 200lb, to match the earlier locomotives; it is

ABOVE Diagram showing the Bulleid paint scheme as applied to an 'H2'. *Madgwick Collection*

said that they then became as fleet-footed as the 'H1s', which were now all superheated as well, so all 11 locomotives were effectively now one class and interchangeable. Shortly before the outbreak of World War 2 a start was made on repainting them in his celebrated malachite green, which suited them rather better than it did most other Southern steam locomotives. This took some time, the first, No 2040 *St Catherine's Point*, receiving the fully lined-out

BELOW In March 1940 the '13s' regained their ability to run over lines barred to them since 1937. By now they were no longer used on express duties, and their future was in some doubt. The Bulleid livery changes took some time to implement, No 2091 being still in Maunsell green when photographed in 1941. It also still retained its Weir pump, but this would shortly be removed, as would the Westinghouse air brake and equipment. The shortening of the chimney was not nearly as noticeable on these tanks as it was on the tender engines, the new design being merely a cut-down version of the original. This last-built '13' was destined also to become the last survivor of the class, finally being withdrawn in May 1952 as BR No 32091. *Ian Allan Library*

ABOVE '13' No 2026 is seen at Uckfield with a train from Lewes to London on 27 May 1939, duties such as this now being their staple work. *Madgwick Collection*

livery in February 1939, the only one so treated before the war.

As a result of the electrification schemes of the 1930s and the restrictions imposed on the line to Tunbridge Wells West the 'I3s' were redistributed throughout the Southern network, some taking up duties on former SECR and LSWR lines. In July 1937 Nos 2088/9 were allocated to Salisbury, where a

year later they were joined by 2084/7. From the summer of 1938 also, following electrification of the Arun Valley line, Nos 2021/2/5/7/9/76/80/90 were employed on Chatham-line trains from the Eastern Section side of Victoria station, although these locomotives remained allocated to Battersea shed for maintenance purposes. Further transfers in 1939 left the 'I3s' spread about the Southern, but three were still based at Tunbridge Wells West, where, in common with others at New Cross, they were employed on the London services and on the Oxted line. Further duties around

Tunbridge Wells West came their way in March 1940 following the strengthening of the weak bridges which had led to the bans in 1937; they were thus able to take over duties from the 'I1Xs', the first of the latter to be withdrawn being No 2600, in October 1944. 'I3s' Nos 2021-8 were now to be found based at Tunbridge Wells West, but this allocation would be reduced in November 1944 by the withdrawal of No 2024, the first of the class to be condemned. One further 'I1X', No 597, would go in December 1946, but the rest of the Atlantic tanks would pass into BR hands.

Despite some Atlantics' being placed in store in the early part of the war, such were the exigencies of the situation that, with effect from November 1940, all six 'H2s' were transferred to Basingstoke shed, on the Western Section. From there they roamed to such far-flung parts of the Southern network as Dorchester and Salisbury, one reportedly being seen as far afield as Yeovil. They did not stay long, however, being transferred in January 1943 to Ashford, whence they worked up to London and across to Margate, Dover and Tonbridge.

No Brighton Atlantics were damaged by the Luftwaffe, but at 12.30pm on 25 May 1943 Brighton was hit by several bombs, five of which landed on the railway. One demolished two arches and one pier at the west end of the London Road viaduct, two arches west of the Preston Road span, leaving the tracks spanning the gap in mid-air. Despite this a temporary repair allowed trains to start using the viaduct again within 24 hours, and in less than a month the service was back to normal. A pair of 'H1' Atlantics (Nos 2037/41) were used to test the temporary repairs, which rather emphasises the downgrading of their importance by this time. Indeed, one of these locomotives, No 2041 *Peverill Point*, was the

first of the Atlantic tender engines to be withdrawn, along with No 2040 *St. Catherine's Point*, in January of the following year, and a month later the remaining 'H1s' and all the 'H2s' were transferred to Brighton shed.

Thus a total of 44 Atlantic tanks (26 Class I3 and 18 Class I1X) and 9 tender engines survived the hostilities. During the war most of the fleet had been repainted plain black with 'Sunshine' lettering, so from 1945 Bulleid wasted no time in reapplying the bright malachite green to the principal passenger locomotives. Although one 'I3', No 2081, had gained malachite in 1940 – which it managed to retain through the conflict – all the rest remained in black for the rest of their lives. Things were different for one of the remaining three 'H1s' and all six 'H2s', however, as, commencing with No 2423 *The Needles* at Eastleigh in June 1945, malachite was restored. Of the earlier class only No 2038 *Portland Bill* was so treated, this locomotive, along with Nos 2422/3/6, being based at Newhaven in 1947 for the Continental boat trains; the line to Newhaven Harbour was electrified from 16 July that year, but electric locomotives would not encroach on the Atlantics' territory for

another couple of years. The Brighton Atlantic prototype, the celebrated No 2037 *Selsey Bill*, would see out its days in plain black, as would the third 'H1' survivor, No 2039 *Hartland Point*.

The story of the Southern Railway was very much one of electrification, and we have seen how the latter affected the careers of the Atlantics. The incredible progress of this policy was abruptly halted on 3 September 1939 by the outbreak of World War 2, from which, some six years later, the railways of Great Britain emerged broken and with all their prewar plans still on hold. We have seen also how the spread of electrification on the Southern pushed many locomotives – especially the Atlantics – out onto more rural lines, but we have yet to consider the effect this had on the railway's locomotive policy.

BELOW No 2023 shows off Bulleid's wartime 'austerity' livery of plain black with 'Sunshine' lettering as it pulls out of Tunbridge Wells West with the 2.12pm train to Victoria, via one of the routes temporarily barred to the 'I3s' before the war. The date, of course, was a wartime secret. *Madgwick Collection*

LEFT AND ABOVE Three photographs that tell their own story. The Lewes line's London Road viaduct was photographed on the afternoon of 25 May 1943 following the air raid at lunchtime. Damage can also be seen to the houses in the background. The second and third photographs (taken the following day!) show the testing of the temporary repairs using two 'H1' Atlantics. No doubt they were the nearest locomotives with few allocated duties – and also, presumably, were considered expendable, should the repairs let them down! No 2041 *Peverill Point* would in any case be scrapped just eight months later. Noodle Books (all)

During his tenure Maunsell had produced various express and mixed-traffic types but no secondary or branch-line passenger classes, while Bulleid's output during his first decade as CME was confined to large numbers of eccentric Pacifics, for express passenger work, and 40 Class Q1 0-6-0 goods engines. The postwar Southern thus had no modern steam locomotives with which to replace the secondary passenger fleet of ex-LSWR 'M7s', ex-SECR 'Hs' and the remaining Brighton Atlantic tanks. The result after much machination was Bulleid's 'Leader' design which had started off as a replacement for the 'M7' design, so he was authorised to produce a modern version of these locomotives. His answer is one of the legends of railway history, his infamous 0-6-6-0 'Leader'.

The 'Leader' project has been the subject of many other histories and would have no relevance to our story were it not for its effect on the third 'H1' survivor, No 2039 *Hartland Point*. Selected to act as a mobile testbed, the

RIGHT No 2425 managed to retain its unlined Bulleid dark-green livery (applied in November 1939) through the war years, gaining the full Malachite splendour in September 1946, a few months after this photograph was taken at New Cross Gate shed. Madgwick Collection

former *La France* was in July 1947 taken into Brighton Works, where it had its front end stripped off to facilitate the fitting of a pair of new cylinders equipped with experimental 'sleeve-valve' gear, six sets of which would feature in the new 'Leader' design. The hapless No 2039 was also disfigured by the fitting of a fabricated wide chimney to go with a multiple-jet blastpipe (the latter at least being well proven on the Pacifics by this time) and outside steam pipes, much of the running-plate around the front being cut away. Emerging thus on 5 November, it made a number of test trips before the end of the year, by which time it was back in works having modifications made.

ABOVE A year after the D-Day landings No 2423 *The Needles* looks absolutely splendid in its new livery of Bulleid malachite green, being pictured thus in the Works Yard at Eastleigh in June 1945. Returning soldiers and others liberated from the gloom of warfare saw this bright livery as a sign of a return to a normal existence. Noodle Books

ABOVE Although 'I3' No 2024 had been withdrawn in September 1944 all the remaining members of the class would see out the conflict. Nos 2080/6 are seen at Brighton on 12 April 1946 sporting a few alterations effected in their later years. No 2080 had been the first of the class to be painted plain black, in 1941, and had a flattened dome, whilst No 2086 had acquired a 'B4' boiler with a round-topped dome which had previously seen service on Nos 2027/76. No 2086 had also received a modified and rounded-roofed cab and retained its Weir pump. *Madgwick Collection*

BELOW In August 1947 'H2' No 2421 *South Foreland* was on show at Eastleigh in its new coat of malachite green. All the 'H2s' and one 'H1' received this livery before the Southern Railway ceased to exist. Note that at this time No 2421 still retained its snifting valves. *Ian Allan Library*

ABOVE AND BELOW No 2425 *Trevose Head* is seen heading south through Clapham Junction with a substantial special, probably a 'Continental Express', in the summer of 1945. It would not gain malachite green until August 1947 but, along with the malachite No 2423 *The Needles*, was nevertheless used on the 'Continental Expresses' following their resumption in January 1945. However, Newhaven shed had Nos 2422/3/6 allocated for these trains from 1947, and the last of these is pictured that summer leaving Newhaven Harbour station on an up relief boat train. Madgwick Collection (both)

ABOVE No 3426 *St Alban's Head* approaches Lewes at Lewes Main Junction signalbox with three standard Southern Railway Van B four-wheeled utility vans from Newhaven to London Victoria. These may well be the front three vehicles of a Continental Boat Train as these trains frequently required considerable additional luggage accommodation to that provided in normal passenger brake coaches. Madgwick Collection

RIGHT Bulleid's 'Leader'-class guinea-pig, the unhappy 'H1' No 2039 *Hartland Point*, is seen at Groombridge during its initial testing phase in late 1947, just before Nationalisation. The transformation seems to go far beyond the cylinders, with mechanical lubricators just below the smokebox and a fabricated chimney taking all the attention. Ian Allan Library

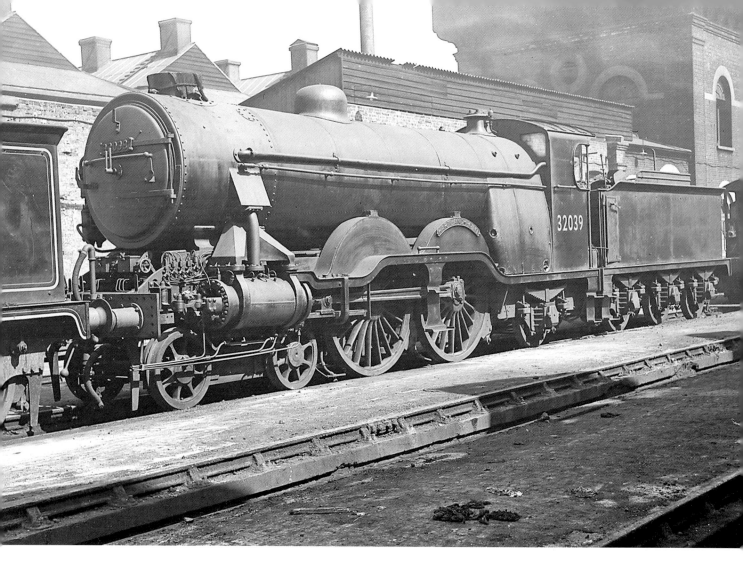

FINALE – BRITISH
RAILWAYS

ABOVE No 32039 is seen waiting in vain for a recall to duty at Brighton between August 1949 and February 1951, when, following BR's abandonment of the extravagant 'Leader' project, it was sent to Eastleigh for scrapping. The subsequent stories in the national press were a public-relations disaster for BR, which was set for many others throughout the 1950s. Railway Correspondence & Travel Society

Within a few days of the formation of British Railways on 1 January 1948 the former London, Brighton & South Coast Railway's once-proud *La France*, now hideously deformed, began a series of test runs between Brighton and Eastbourne to gather data for O. V. S. Bulleid's forthcoming 'Leader'-class locomotives, five of which were under construction at Brighton Works. It appears to have worked quite successfully until 19 December 1948, when it fractured the right-hand valve rocker. It was quickly repaired and the tests continued, its first public outing in rebuilt form coming on 14 March 1949, when it worked the Hastings–Birkenhead inter-regional train from Brighton to Redhill (the old Southern Railway being now the Southern Region of BR). Following that it was taken back out of service for improvements to be made to the valve gear and for a boiler change.

In the spring of 1949 the first 'Leader', No 36001, was released for trials, following which the 'H1' was no longer needed. In anticipation of a return to normal service *Hartland Point* (which name the locomotive

had retained for the duration of the tests) was given a fresh coat of plain black complete with BR number 32039, being noted thus outside Brighton Works at the end of August. However, it never left and, like partly completed 'Leaders' Nos 36002-5, rusted away until towed to Eastleigh in February 1951. The 'Leader' project had in the meantime become a hot topic in the national press, BR having allowed testing of No 36001 to continue until 2 November 1950, when the project was cancelled. A further insight into the 'Leader' project and its relevance to the story of the Brighton Atlantics can be found in Appendix III.

No 32039 would finally be scrapped in March 1951, the remaining two 'H1s', Nos 32037/8, following suit in July, but more alarming for admirers of these magnificent machines was the withdrawal in May 1949 of 'H2' No 2423 *The Needles*, which never even received its BR number; it went to the breakers still sporting its 1945 fully lined-out malachite-green livery. The remaining five 'H2s' would receive BR's lined-out mixed-traffic black, although they were definitely not mixed-traffic locomotives, and indeed this livery was officially described as 'Secondary Passenger & Mixed Traffic Lined Black'. The thinning of the ranks of the Atlantics was primarily a result of the loss of some of their primary boat-train duties at Newhaven, the Bullied/ Raworth 'Hornby' electric locomotives taking over the main duties from 15 May 1949, although the old-timers were retained for reliefs and extra turns.

Plain black remained the colour for the 'I1X' 4-4-2Ts. Ten of the 18 that had passed into BR stock were withdrawn during 1948, but the remaining eight lasted for another three years as the effects of the 'Leader' *débâcle* began to bite and BR had to come up with an alternative scheme to replace the old Southern tanks. The survivors would ultimately be replaced by LMS-designed 'Mickey Mouse' Class 2 2-6-2 tanks, but not before the appearance of No 32,005, the former No 2005 emerging thus from repaint; the comma was overpainted before the locomotive's release to traffic, but with the passage of time the patch wore out, and the comma gradually reappeared! All other members of the class met the end still displaying their Southern numbers.

In BR ownership the remaining 'I3s' initially fared better than the 'I1Xs', all 26 surviving until the beginning of 1950, when, beginning with No S2025 in January, a steady stream of them was withdrawn, seven more following in 1950, and a further 17 in 1951. That left just one, No 32091, the last built, which soldiered on until May 1952. All but No S2025 (the 'S' indicative of a temporary numbering system employed by BR, the former No 2025 being the only 'I3' so treated) ultimately received BR numbers in the 32xxx series, in addition to which Nos 32028/9/75/7/8/9/81/6/91 were painted in the full lined black. They were replaced by examples of another LMS tank-engine design, this time Charles Fairburn's Class 4 2-6-4T, three batches of which were built at Brighton from 1950.

Withdrawal of the final 'I1X' and 'I3' 4-4-2 tanks left the five surviving 'H2s' as the last Atlantics in BR service, having outlasted the final Ivatt Atlantics (*i.e.* those that were actually ascribed to him) on the Eastern Region, of which No 62822 was the last to go, in November 1950. Happily, upon withdrawal in July 1947, the 'C1' prototype, GNR No 251

ABOVE Only two 'H1s' remained in general service in early BR days, of which the class pioneer, *Selsey Bill*, became BR No 32037 in April 1949 but remained plain black, without any evidence of ownership, as seen here at East Croydon later that year. The order for its withdrawal came in July 1951, just five months after No 32039 was condemned. Madgwick Collection

(LNER No 2800), was retained for preservation – an event that was to prove extremely significant in the history of the Brighton locomotives. Another LNER connection involved the special train to the Farnborough Air Show on 7 July 1950, headed by No 32421 *South Foreland* because the stock comprised a rake of ex-Great Eastern Railway air-braked coaches, the Brighton Atlantics being by now the only air-braked passenger tender engines on the Southern Region.

ABOVE AND BELOW No 2038 passed into BR stock in the malachite-green livery it had gained on overhaul in September 1947 at Eastleigh and, other than receiving its BR number (32038), would work out its last years in that form, being condemned along with No 32037 in July 1951. Madgwick Collection, Railway Correspondence & Travel Society

ABOVE BR inherited two types of Brighton Atlantic tank as well as two classes of tender engine. Although 10 of the surviving '11Xs' went in 1948 seven of the remaining eight continued in traffic until 1951. Here we take a last look at No 2002 on shed at Brighton, still displaying its SR number and in SR livery as late as 15 May 1951, just two months from withdrawal.
Railway Correspondence & Travel Society

The five survivors, which were repainted in BR lined black between May 1949 (No 32421) and September 1951 (32424), now had little scheduled work and spent periods of time in store. Slated for withdrawal in 1951, they were reprieved because, amongst other things, Brighton shed was having trouble keeping its allocation of Bulleid Light Pacifics active; sometimes all of them (between five and seven locomotives, the allocation changing frequently) would be out of action! As their principal work was on the through trains to Bournemouth, Plymouth and Cardiff the 'H2s' were frequently called upon to deputise. Throughout 1951 the latter saw a variety of duties, including Newhaven boat trains, parcels work from Brighton, substitutions for

Fairburn tanks on the Oxted lines and ventures onto the Western Division (Sections having become Divisions under BR) to Bournemouth on a number of occasions.

By 1952 the Atlantics had become celebrities, and from then on they were called upon to work a number of special trains, the most notable that year being two to celebrate the centenary of Brighton Works, on 5 and 19 October, each organised by the Railway Correspondence & Travel Society (RCTS) and running as the 'Southern Belle'. Both trains were all-Pullman, running to the 'fast' schedule down and up the Brighton main line. On the first run No 32424 *Beachy Head*, manned by Newhaven men, provided the

power, whilst on the second a Brighton crew had charge of No 32425 *Trevose Head*. As noted earlier, Brighton Works had been established in the 1840s, so the 'centenary' specials marked the 100th anniversary not of its opening (which would have been during World War 2) but of the construction of its first locomotive. On both the 5th and the 19th 'Terrier' No 32636 worked a shuttle to Kemp Town, which station had closed to passengers as long ago as 1933 but had remained open for goods (and would prove a popular destination for railtours until its final demise in 1971). The 'Southern Belle' timetable was as follows (the trains running within a minute of the schedule on both occasions):

Miles	Station/passing point*	Time southbound (am)	Time northbound (pm)
0.0	Victoria	10.14 (dep)	5.28 (arr)
4.9	Balham Junction*	10.23	5.20
10.0	Windmill Bridge Junction*	10.29	5.14
15.0	Coulsdon North	10.35	5.08
21.9	Earlswood	10.43	5.00½
29.6	Three Bridges	10.51	4.53
38.0	Haywards Heath	10.59	4.44
41.1	Keymer Junction*	11.03	4.41
50.9	Brighton	11.14 (arr)	2.28 (dep)

ABOVE AND BELOW Lasting a little longer than the '11Xs' in active service, the '13s' were well covered in their final days. Their work still included trains to London, and Nos 32027, still with 'Southern' on the tank sides, and 32082, with 'British Railways' in full, were recorded at Clapham Junction in 1949, the latter powering the 11.8 London Victoria to Oxted and beyond on 2 July.

Ian Allan Library, C. C. B. Herbert, Madgwick Collection

ABOVE There was quite a variety of liveries to be seen on the '13s' in their last days. The first of a series of four pictures shows No 32028 at Eastleigh in 1949, fully lined out in black but devoid of ownership details. Ian Allan Library

BELOW Unlined and apparently ownerless, No 32076 heads a set of carmine-and-cream ex-LMS stock – including a brand-new 'Porthole' Brake Third – on the lineal descendant of the 'Sunny South Express' (the Birmingham New Street–Hastings restaurant-car train) at Southerham Lifting Bridge, south of Lewes, on 22 July 1950. S. C. Nash/Madgwick Collection

ABOVE No 32022, in shiny but plain black, displays the early-style BR totem at Tunbridge Wells West on 7 October 1950.
H. C. Casserley/Madgwick Collection

BELOW In weathered and dull plain black, No 32030 stands at Tonbridge on 14 May 1951. Railway Correspondence & Travel Society

ABOVE AND BELOW The last-built '13' was also the last survivor, the fully-lined-out and crested No 32091 being seen approaching East Grinstead High Level from London in 1951 and then on shed at Brighton on 5 October the same year, the day before No 32086 was condemned and a matter of 19 days before it became the last of its class, when No 32075 succumbed. No 32091 would soldier on into May 1952. Madgwick Collection, Railway Correspondence & Travel Society

As the 1950s progressed Brighton's Bulleids were still giving trouble, so Atlantics continued to take turn and turn about with them on ventures onto the Western Division. In the late autumn of 1952 No 32421 *South Foreland* worked around 70% of the Bournemouth turn, while No 32426 *St. Alban's Head* was used on at least four occasions. By May 1953 No 32421 was looking decidedly down at heel when photographed at Fratton shed and would be the only 'H2' to be repainted three times in BR days, initially in May 1949, again in November 1951 and yet again in October 1954; Nos 32424 and 32426 would be repainted twice, and the other pair just once.

Almost every move the Atlantics made was now being recorded, as their celebrity status continued to grow. In 1954 a number of runs were made on the Oxted lines, as well as more boat trains. The following year would prove to be a vintage one, featuring yet more railtours, of which the most notable were the 'Hampshireman' of 6 February, headed by a suitably cleaned-up No 32421 *South Foreland* from Waterloo via Barnes, Chertsey and Woking to Guildford, and the 'Wealden Limited' of 14 August, which from Lewes was worked by No 32426 *St. Alban's Head* over the then closed Bluebell line via Horsted Keynes. Both were organised by the RCTS. Timings for the Atlantic-hauled segments were as follows:

'Hampshireman'

Miles	Station/passing point*	Time (am)
0.00	Waterloo	9.45 (dep)
3.71	Clapham Junction	9.52
10.52	Brentford Central	10.08
14.11	Hounslow Junction*	10.16
20.07	Staines Central	10.28
26.62	Chertsey	10.40
30.05	Byfleet Junction*	10.47
34.10	Woking	10.53
40.09	Guildford	11.03 (arr)

'

Wealden Limited'

Miles	Station/passing point*	Time (pm)
129.33	Lewes	4.56 (dep)
132.52	Culver Junction*	5.03
137.16	Newick & Chailey	5.12
143.40	Horsted Keynes	5.26 (arr)
		5.36 (dep)
149.68	East Grinstead (Low Level)	5.52
153.50	Lingfield	5.58
156.45	Crowhurst North Junction*	6.03
159.51	Oxted	6.08
167.53	Sanderstead	6.22
168.56	South Croydon	6.25
169.48	East Croydon	6.28
170.09	Windmill Bridge Junction*	6.30
174.28	Forest Hill	6.44
177.04	New Cross Gate	6.51 (arr)
		7.16 (dep)
177.65	Old Kent Road Junction*	7.22
178.71	Peckham Rye	7.28
182.64	Battersea Park	7.37
184.05	Victoria	7.40 (arr)

One rather unusual working on 21 August 1955, a week after the 'Wealden Limited', saw No 32424 *Beachy Head* being used on a two-coach Invalid Special from Victoria to Crowborough. The following month the type's sojourn at Newhaven came to an end, the shed being closed with effect from 19 September, whereupon all of the surviving Atlantics congregated at Brighton, just across the tracks from where they had been built some 44 years earlier.

The year 1956 was one of unexpected problems for the survivors, an inheritance from their Ivatt progenitors. Ivatt's bogie design was very effective in terms of improving the riding of the locomotives, and Gresley continued to use what was fundamentally the same design for all his express passenger designs which had a front bogie. Amongst these was the solitary Class W1 4-6-4, 'the A4-that-wasn't', a rebuild of his so-called 'Hush-Hush' Yarrow-boilered high-pressure water-tube No 10000 of 1929. On 1 September 1955 the locomotive had just departed Peterborough when the front bogie frame broke, causing the train to be derailed. Investigating the cause of the accident took some time, but when the report was finally published it recommended that all locomotives with a similar design of bogie be inspected, to see whether they were suffering similar defects. It took some time for this process to trickle through to the Southern Region, but in May 1956 all five 'H2s' were taken out of service for inspection.

Nos 32421/6 were found to have faulty bogie frames and remained out of service, whilst No 32422 was allowed to return to

work, but only on light duties. Nos 32424/5 were cleared and returned to work, but it was decided that the two with faulty frames should be withdrawn, this taking effect in August. No 32422 suffered a broken left cylinder just before it was to work a ramblers' special and was withdrawn in September, while No 32425 was also found to have worn cylinders, and this, together with cracks in the frames, led to its withdrawal the same month. However, that was not the end for this great machine, as it was taken to Slade Green to be used as a steam generator to heat the electric depot, from 30 December 1956 until April 1957, after which it would play its part in the final act of the Brighton Atlantic story.

Thus No 32424 *Beachy Head* became officially the last British Atlantic in BR service. It should be pointed out that there were still a few Atlantic *tanks* on BR's books, but, despite the fact that this book has traced the history of *all* Brighton Atlantics, including the tanks, to most enthusiasts the term 'Atlantic' suggests a tender engine. In any case, No 32424 was certainly the last Brighton Atlantic! During 1957 it worked intermittently on the Bournemouth through train and on 24 February headed an LCGB railtour, the 'Southern Counties Limited', from Kew East Junction via Lewisham and Sanderstead to Horsted Keynes on the revived (but not yet preserved) Bluebell line. Curiously, this was its only railtour outing in 1957, after which it was stored at Brighton, only to be steamed again on 18 June, when it blew its left-hand cylinder cover off. Having been towed back to Brighton from Slade Green in April, No 32425 now performed its part in the final act, donating a cylinder cover, and *Beachy Head* escaped the torch one more time. Following this Lazarus moment it worked a number of other interesting trains, including on Saturday 24 August the 10.51 Hastings–Leicester as far as Kensington Addison Road and 12.35 return from Leicester, on Sunday 8 September the 11.25 from Brighton to Redhill and North Camp and on Saturday 21 December the 10.5am Special Vans from Bricklayers Arms to Brighton. So it was that No 32424 was still in existence at the close of 1957, a year which had been expected to mark its demise – something that was postponed because the

ABOVE The Bulleid/Raworth electric locomotives, affectionately known as 'Hornbys', took over the principal Newhaven 'Continental Expresses' with effect from 15 May 1949 – a clear indication that the remaining 'H1s' and 'H2s' were living on borrowed time. Photographed on 2 June, the last-built of the trio, No 20003, with '4-SUB'-style front end, leads a train of Maunsell stock painted in a uniform new BR livery (save for a solitary Pullman near the rear) past Clapham Junction.
C. C. B. Herbert/Madgwick Collection

RCTS had requested its use on the Victoria–Newhaven leg of its proposed 'Sussex Coast Limited' tour, scheduled for 13 April 1958.

The year 1958 would go down in railway history as the last in which a British Atlantic express locomotive worked on the nation's railway network. On 9 April, having been prepared at Brighton, No 32424 was steamed once again and despatched to London at the head of a London Bridge van train. Five days later the RCTS special left London Victoria at 10.25am and ran non-stop to Newhaven Harbour station, which was reached at 11.46, one minute late after a number of signal checks and stops. There the locomotive was released from the train, which was taken back to Newhaven Town by No 32640, one of the long-lasting Stroudley 'Terriers', retained at this time to work the Hayling Island branch. BR Standard Class 4 2-6-4 tank No 80154, the last steam locomotive built at Brighton, then took the train on to Brighton, where it was joined by *Beachy Head* at the works.

Miles	Station/passing point*	Time (am)
00.00	Victoria	10.25 (dep)
02.57	Clapham Junction	10.31
04.69	Balham Junction*	10.35
10.04	Windmill Bridge Junction*	10.42
10.45	East Croydon	10.43
15.03	Coulsdon North	10.50½
17.60	Quarry Tunnel (north end)*	10.53½
21.72	Earlswood	10.59
26.01	Horley	11.03½
29.45	Three Bridges	11.07½
31.75	Balcombe Tunnel Junction*	11.10
38.02	Haywards Heath	11.17½
41.13	Keymer Junction*	11.21½
44.65	Plumpton	11.25
50.20	Lewes	11.33½
56.38	Newhaven Town	11.43
56.65	Newhaven Harbour	11.45 (arr)

One somewhat mournful duty was left. On 24 April 1958 No 32424 coupled up to the 7.28am Lancing–Eastleigh ECS train and set off for the old LSWR works in the Hampshire town of Eastleigh (itself a creation of the railway), where its fire was dropped for the last time. The locomotive still looked absolutely splendid and ready to work its next train, but this was not to be, and it was broken up the following month. The failure to secure the preservation of The Last British Atlantic is said to have been the result of the previous preservation of two of its progenitors, the Great Northern Nos 990 and 251. BR considered that the retention of those two engines effectively covered the Atlantic type sufficiently in the historic sense, so it could not

justify another almost-identical machine in its preservation programme.

Before concluding this chapter it is worth comparing *Beachy Head*'s longevity with that of another top-link express locomotive – an example of the Pacific design, which supplanted the Atlantic. The longest-lived British Pacific (in terms of its working life, excluding preservation) was the LNER's *Flying Fox*, which was built in April 1923, the fourth of a batch of 10 locomotives which included the immortal *Flying Scotsman*. When retired in December 1964 as BR No 60106 it had thus been at work for 42 years and eight months; when *Beachy Head* entered Eastleigh Works that day in April 1958 it had been at work for 46 years and eight months.

ABOVE By 1950 the 'H2s' were being noticed by railway enthusiasts across the country, and most of their work from this time appears to have been recorded on film. On 30 May No 2425 *Trevose Head* **was recorded at Sanderstead on an Oxted-line London train. It would receive its BR number and fully lined-out black livery in October that year.** Madgwick Collection

ABOVE AND LEFT No 32421 *South Foreland*, which was to be repainted three times in lined black, was active during 1950 with no indication of ownership, being seen thus at Hurst Green on a set of ex-SECR 'Birdcage' stock and again at Farnborough on 7 July with a train of ex-Great Eastern stock on a special to the Farnborough Air Show. Madgwick Collection, Ian Allan Library

RIGHT The year 1951 was one of contrasts for the 'H2s', which continued to be used on Newhaven boat trains when additional workings were operated. Here No 32425 *Trevose Head* gets underway from the East Sussex port on 22 June.
S. Teasdale/Madgwick Collection

So the story of the Brighton Atlantics would seem to end with the demise of No 32424. But, to repeat an oft-quoted line, 'Perchance it is not dead but sleepeth.'*

* These words [– themselves an adaptation of those spoken by Christ when raising the daughter of the president of the synagogue, as quoted in the Authorized Version of the Bible (Matthew 9.24 and Mark 5.39) –] were written by Captain Thomas Alfred Woolf RN and formed part of the inscription left on a wreath on the stop-blocks at Barnstaple Town station following the closure in 1935 of the Lynton & Barnstaple Railway, which has since been revived.

ABOVE On 4 July 1951 No 32421 *South Foreland* still exhibited no form of ownership on its tender as it left Brighton with the 5.30pm parcels train to London Bridge. It would gain a further coat of lined black at Eastleigh in November.

P. J. Lynch/Madgwick Collection

FACING PAGE TOP An unusual view – almost inevitably including No 32421 *South Foreland* – of the approaches to East Croydon from the front guard's van of the 5.40pm London Bridge–East Grinstead train features what was the largest signal gantry on the former Brighton system.

P. J. Lynch/Madgwick Collection

FACING PAGE BOTTOM *North Foreland* – No 32422 – was not quite as ubiquitous as its southerly sister but did reach Bournemouth on more than one occasion in 1951, being recorded at Boscombe station on the return leg of the Brighton–Bournemouth through train on 5 May.

Railway Correspondence & Travel Society

ABOVE On 28 November 1951 No 32421 also visited Bournemouth, being recorded shortly before the train's scheduled departure from Bournemouth Central at **1.55pm.** Railway Correspondence & Travel Society

BELOW AND RIGHT The highlight of 1952 was undoubtedly the RCTS-promoted 'Southern Belle', which ran twice, on 5 and 19 October. The first run featured No 32424 *Beachy Head*, which locomotive is seen in these three photographs successively awaiting its train outside Victoria, running through Clapham Junction with the Pullmans and preparing for its return **at Brighton.** Railway Correspondence & Travel Society (2), E. D. Bruton/Madgwick Collection

ABOVE AND BELOW Two weeks after *Beachy Head*'s day in the limelight came the turn of No 32425 *Trevose Head*, here seen first outside at Stewarts Lane shed and then running along the Brighton main line at Wandsworth Common. Ian Allan Library, Madgwick Collection

ABOVE Not to be left out, No 32421 *South Foreland* was photographed on shed at Brighton in 1952, by now sporting signs of BR ownership. Madgwick Collection

BELOW Following its exposure in 1952 No 32425 *Trevose Head* was photographed rather less in 1953, some of which it spent in store. Ian Allan Library

ABOVE AND BELOW *South Foreland*'s 1951 repaint at Eastleigh must have been a pretty shoddy effort, as by May 1953 when photographed in steam at Fratton it was rusting badly and looked ready for the torch. *Trevose Head*, on one of its adventures away from home, looked in far better state when photographed that same month at Brockenhurst, with the Bournemouth through train.
Colour-Rail BRS1405, BRS991

ABOVE AND BELOW *Trevose Head* was back in the limelight in 1954, working a number of trains on the Oxted lines. Here it is seen first at Sanderstead on the 5.40pm from London Bridge during the summer and then in September pouring out plenty of black stuff as it approaches Upper Warlingham station with the 6.10pm from Victoria. R. Russell/Madgwick Collection (both)

ABOVE AND LEFT The first of three
notable adventures for the remaining
Brighton Atlantics in 1955 saw No 32421
South Foreland to the fore again, heading
the RCTS 'Hampshireman' from Waterloo
as far as Guildford on 6 February,
the second view showing it between
Feltham and Ashford (Middx).
Author, Madgwick Collection

LEFT AND BELOW The 'Wealden Limited', another RCTS tour, had No 32426 *St. Alban's Head* to haul it over some traditional Brighton metals, and it was photographed at (amongst many other places) Lewes after taking over the train and Horsted Keynes on the then closed Bluebell line. Colour-Rail BRS664, 340039

BELOW The third adventure, on 21 August 1955, saw No 32424 *Beachy Head* take an invalid special from London to Crowborough, the train continuing thence as empty carriage stock to Lewes. It was filmed with the ECS apparently working 'wrong road' near South Malling, a result of engineering works on the down line. The invalid saloon is an ex-South Eastern Railway vehicle.
S. C. Nash/Madgwick Collection

ABOVE On 29 April 1956, seven months after the East Coast accident that was to have a significant bearing on the future of the surviving Brighton Atlantics, No 32425 *Trevose Head* was looking spry as it left Bournemouth on the now 2.2pm return working of the Bournemouth through train. Just a few days later the report on the accident involving Gresley 'W1' No 60700 would lead to the withdrawal of two of the five survivors and, shortly afterwards, to that of No 32425 itself, due to cracks in the frames and worn cylinders – faults that would no doubt have been corrected had it not been for the question marks hanging over the class's future. Railway Correspondence & Travel Society

FACING PAGE TOP Seen outside Brighton Works in May 1956 are Nos 32426 *St. Alban's Head* and 32422 *South Foreland*, awaiting inspections which will seal their fate. No 32426 was found to have faults and would never return to service, whilst No 32422, despite having its motion taken down at this time, would return to light duties but was to last only until it broke its left-hand cylinder in September. Ian Allan Library

FACING PAGE BOTTOM The saddest sight: No 32426 *St. Alban's Head* being dismembered inside Brighton Works following the inspection which revealed a faulty front bogie frame. Ian Allan Library

ABOVE The saddest sight repeated: No 32425 *Trevose Head* being stripped, also at Brighton, although this locomotive survived into 1957 through its use as a stationary boiler for Slade Green electric depot, finally being sent to Eastleigh for scrapping in August of that year after donating its left-hand cylinder cover to No 32424 *Beachy Head*. Ian Allan Library

BELOW Surprisingly, in view of its 'last' status, No 32424 *Beachy Head* was used on only one railtour in 1957, this being the LCGB's 'Southern Counties Limited' of 24 February, from Kew East to the Bluebell line. It was photographed at Selsdon in rather gloomy conditions. Madgwick Collection

RIGHT AND BELOW The story of No 32424 *Beachy Head*'s final railtour on 13 April 1958 has gone down in railway folklore. In this series of five photographs the locomotive is seen first at Brighton being prepared for the event, then at the platform ends of Brighton station, upon arrival at Victoria and, finally, on the turntable at Newhaven shed, its old home and for three decades the provider of work for the Atlantics. Colour-Rail BRS220, 340947, Railway Correspondence & Travel Society, Colour-Rail 340951, 394349

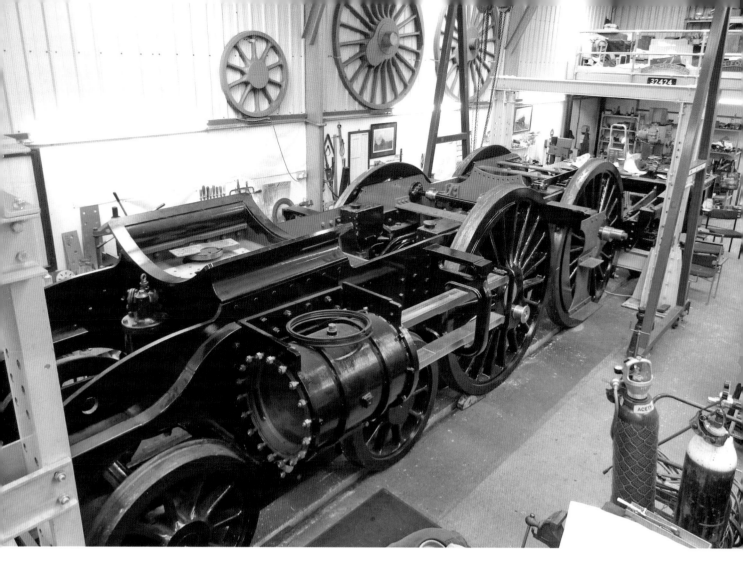

CHAPTER 11

REINCARNATION

ABOVE The new Brighton Atlantic is seen in the late summer of 2014 under construction in 'Atlantic House' on the Bluebell Railway. Note the smokebox numberplate in the background – the locomotive will be finished in BR lined black as No 32424, as *Beachy Head* was when she was scrapped in 1958. Although some at Eastleigh tried to save her, photographs of her in her partially cut condition have proven invaluable to the new build as they show details hitherto unseen. Only about 50 drawings from an original set of 270 have survived. Most have been redrawn and other parts redesigned by the Brighton Atlantic Group. They have produced over 500 working drawings plus the same number again of design sketches and trial arrangements or detail drawings. The build team is small, two men for two days per week plus one for three days per week. In addition they have one volunteer for one day per week and another ace turner for a half day per week. Two of the trust-funded staff work an extra volunteer day each week. There is also a backup support team who do all the less glamorous but very vital jobs, fundraising, book keeping, magazine editor etc., all volunteers amounting to about eight people who assist as and when needed. That is the important bit and the reason for the Group's success – as they say, 'It's a team effort – primadonnas need not apply!' Details can be found at http://www.bluebell-railway.co.uk/bluebell/locos/atlantic/

Despite its reputation amongst railway enthusiasts of the latter half of the 20th century as 'just an electric railway' and the fact that it played no part in steam-locomotive development following the Grouping, the Brighton celebrated a number of important landmarks, demonstrating that it was, in many ways, the true pioneer of railway preservation, and the years immediately following the scrapping of *Beachy Head* would see a significant increase in Brighton activity. First and foremost, in 1959, was the 50th anniversary of the Stephenson Locomotive Society, the first railway-preservation organisation. Some 32 years earlier it had secured the preservation of the first of William Stroudley's classic 'B'-class 0-4-2s express locomotives, No 214 *Gladstone*, the only Brighton tender engine to escape the scrapman's torch. In addition to the historical importance, the actual preservation of the locomotive had marked a 'first' for railway preservation as its saving by the members of the society was the first instance of preservation of a locomotive by a private body. The following is an extract from the society's own record of this magnificent achievement:

Gladstone was built in 1882, entered service at Brighton in January 1883 and was withdrawn in December 1926, after running 1,346,918 miles.

The SLS had been founded at Croydon in 1909 and there was a strong interest in Brighton locomotives among the early members. Therefore in 1926 as many older locomotives were being withdrawn by the Southern Railway, the Society felt that something of the LB&SCR should be preserved and negotiations were put in hand for the purchase of 'Gladstone'.

In the Society's circular of 11 February 1927 the then President of the SLS, J. N. Maskelyne, wrote:

"It is with utmost pleasure that, on behalf of the Council, I am able to announce that preliminary negotiations for the celebrated LB&SCR locomotive 'Gladstone' are now completed. This engine has been withdrawn from service and is at Brighton works, where the work of restoring her to her original condition and painting her in the famous old yellow livery is to be put in hand immediately. I

am sure that all our members will appreciate fully the kindness of the Southern Railway Co. in helping us to carry out such a scheme as this, certainly the most ambitious scheme ever undertaken by our Society. We are, also, deeply indebted to the London & North Eastern Railway Co. who have offered to find space for the 'Gladstone' in their Railway Museum at York until such time as accommodation can be found in London, possibly at South Kensington Museum, in the course of a few years.

"There is no need for me to enlarge upon the reasons as to why this engine is being preserved; it is enough if I say here that she represents the unique achievement of a unique Locomotive Engineer whose influence upon Locomotive Engineering generally can still be noted at the present time. That 'Gladstone' was a sound proposition in the first place, designed with the utmost care and almost uncanny foresight, is proved by the fact that her term of usefulness has amounted to forty-four years. From now on she will remain the property of the Society, and I am certain that every member will agree that she is a possession of which we may well be proud, and an asset of which the value will increase with the passing years."

The item was followed by an appeal for funds, which were successfully raised and on 31 May 1927 it was ceremonially handed over to the LNER for safe keeping in the old Railway Museum at York, where it can still be seen today.

In 1959 the Society celebrated its Golden Jubilee and it wished to have 'Gladstone' in the best of condition to mark the event. Society Officers visited York to find there was nothing radically wrong with the engine, but it was in obvious need of a repaint. The price quoted by the British Transport Commission, which was now responsible for the (old) York Museum was beyond the Society's means and therefore the time had come to offer 'Gladstone' to the BTC with its other historical relics.

The locomotive was therefore repainted under the supervision of Society members who had researched the accurate colouring

and lining used in Brighton days; it was possibly the most accurate restoration of any preserved locomotive in Europe at the time. 'Gladstone' was formally handed over to the BTC at York on 18 September 1959.

With the transfer of relics from the former BTC, 'Gladstone' became part of the National Collection and was moved to the new National Railway Museum at York when it opened in 1975.

The Brighton connection with railway preservation remained strong, and a new generation of enthusiasts who had grown up after World War 2 vowed to try to preserve more of their railway memories than simply locomotives. This was at a time when British Railways was trying to eliminate steam and to close unremunerative lines. In the SLS's Golden Jubilee year a new society was set up to attempt to purchase part of the Brighton's line from East Grinstead to Lewes, which had closed in 1958 for the second time after BR's initial attempt to close it in 1955 had been thwarted by a local user – one Margery Bessemer, of Chailey. She discovered that in the 1877 and 1878 Acts which had authorised the building of the line a clause related to the 'Statutory Line' and forbade closure without a new Act of Parliament to repeal those Acts, and demanded British Railways reinstate services. On 7 August 1956 British Railways reopened the line, with trains stopping at stations mentioned in the Acts. British Railways took the case to the House of Commons in 1957, resulting in a public inquiry. British Railways were censured, but later the Transport Commission was able to persuade Parliament to repeal the special section of the Act. By this means the line was finally closed on 17 March 1958.

On 15 March 1959 a group that included future President of Society Bernard Holden, a fourth-generation career railwayman born in the Brighton railway-station house at Barcombe, on the Bluebell line, met in Ardingly to form the Lewes & East Grinstead Railway Preservation Society. The society elected John Leeroy as its first chairman, and £940 was raised through donation. In response to a vote held at the meeting the society later changed its name to the Bluebell Railway Preservation Society.

The society's initial aim was to reopen the whole line from East Grinstead to Culver

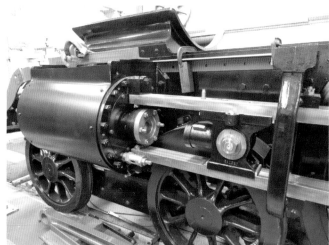
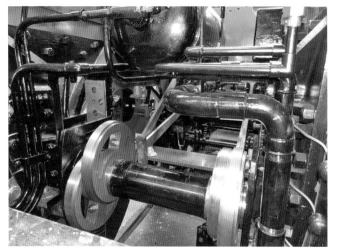
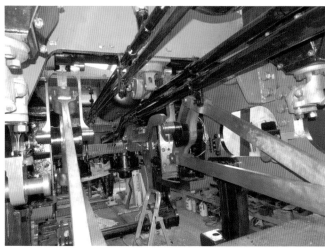

Junction as a commercial venture, but these plans came to nothing; the society failed to buy the whole line, and most local residents weren't interested. The committee then recommended that the stretch of track between Sheffield Park and Horsted Keynes be run as a tourist attraction, with vintage locomotives and stock operated by unpaid volunteer staff, and a bid was submitted to British Railways which was accepted, the society purchasing the line from just south of Horsted Keynes and leasing access to the station, which at that time still had a BR electric service running through to Haywards Heath.

The acquisition and reopening of the Bluebell Railway in 1960 can be seen as the first evidence that railway preservation in its most literal sense, that of preserving a *railway* rather than simply preserving railway artefacts, was feasible. The Bluebell Railway was the first standard-gauge former (secondary) main line to be preserved in the entire world and became the blueprint for what is the

highly successful heritage-railway industry of modern times.

Not only was the Bluebell a Brighton-built line; it also boasted a number of locomotives from the Brighton itself, having saved two Stroudley 'Terriers' and the only surviving Billinton 'Radial' tank of Class E4. The locomotive fleet grew throughout the rest of the 20th century, and the Bluebell Railway itself was gradually extended until it was once again reconnected to the national network, at East Grinstead, in 2013. But that locomotive fleet, boasting many steam locomotives from across the nation, had no 'local' star. The Bluebell Society had been formed just too late for *Beachy Head*.

In 1986 two members of the Engine Shed Society – Nick Piggott, then editor of *Steam Railway* magazine, and a colleague – visited Boulton Paul's sawmill at Maldon in Essex, where four former steam-locomotive boilers had been installed to provide power for the

sawmills. Two of these were identified as being from GNR Ivatt 'Large Atlantics' (LNER Class C1). One was completely worn out, but the other was in restorable condition, and a subsequent article in *Steam Railway* led to a suggestion that it might form the basis of an exciting project that would ultimately see a Brighton Atlantic running once again on Brighton metals. As we have seen, a GNR 'Large Atlantic' boiler was almost identical to that of a Brighton Atlantic, and the Bluebell Railway was persuaded to form a 'Bluebell Railway Atlantic Group' to acquire the good boiler and use it in the construction of a new 'H2'. The decision was taken to re-create the most famous one of all, so the seventh member of the 'H2' class will be a replica of No 32424 *Beachy Head* as she was back in 1958.

If a steam locomotive can be said to exist once its frames have been cut and assembled, the new locomotive came into being in October 2007, and by 2014 the cylinders

These photographs by Fred Bailey illustrate the progress at the time of going to press. A new-build locomotive requires a massive amount of parts created from scratch. Most items have been manufactured on site (with the obvious exceptions of large castings and items such as wheels and frames). The yellow-painted jacks required to raise the frames in order to position the wheels were designed and built in-house to suit the available space and to save on crane hire, as these can be used any time, and will be handy for future new build projects! Even small items take a great deal of work – such as the handmade screws that are inside the semi-plug piston valve heads (stored in a matchbox!) and the complex parts for the reversing handle copied from the original design. The latter has a very tricky double dovetail slot and matching component that is the catch that engages the 'gearwheel' seen just behind the handle itself.

were in place, along with much of the motion, and the frames had been lifted onto the brand-new driving wheels. More than a century after the first six 'H2s' were placed in traffic, it was no longer a case of 'if' a new Atlantic would ever run but 'when'.

The story of the Brighton Atlantics is not yet over...

APPENDICES

I: Classes

Class H (Class H1 from 1 January 1907)
5 locomotives in class

Numbers:
37-41 (LBSCR)
B37-41 (SR to 1931)
2037-41 (SR from 1931)
32039-41 (BR)

Weight in working order:	67 tons 0 cwt (engine)
Boiler pressure:	200lb sq in
Cylinders:	Nos 37/38/40/41 18½in x 26in
	No 39: 19in x 2in
Tractive effort:	Nos 37/38/40/41 19,028 lb
	No 39 20,070lb
Driving-wheel diameter:	6ft 7½in
Valve gear:	Stephensons, slide valves
Delivered:	No 37 – 10 December 1905
	No 38 – 24 December 1905
	No 39 – 23 January 1906
	No 40 – 2 February 1906
	No 41 –19 February 1906
Withdrawn:	No 2040 – January 1944
	No 2041 – March 1944
	No 32039 – February 1951
	No 32037 – July 1951
	No 32038 – July 1951

Class I1/I1X
20 locomotives in class

Numbers:
1-10/595-604 (LBSCR)
B1-10/595-604 (SR to 1931)
2001-10/595-604 (SR from 1931)
32001-10/595/6/8/9/601-4 (BR, not all carried)

Weight in working order*:	I1 – 1st series, nos 595-604 68 tons 6 cwt
	– 2nd series, nos 1-10 68 tons 10 cwt
	I1X – 1st series 71 tons 14 cwt
	– 2nd series 71 tons 18 cwt*
Boiler pressure:	170lb sq in (initially 170 then 180 as I1X)
Cylinders:	17½in x 26in
Tractive effort:	17,430lb
Driving-wheel diameter:	5ft 6in

Valve gear:	Stephensons, slide valves
Delivered:	No 595 – September 1906
	No 596 – November 1906
	No 597 – December 1906
	No 598 – January 1907
	No 599 – February 1907
	No 600 – March 1907
	Nos 601/2/4 – April 1907
	Nos 1/603 – June 1907
	Nos 2/3 – July 1907
	No 4 – August 1907
	No 5 – September 1907
	Nos 6/7 – October 1907
	No 8 – November 1907
	No2 9/10 – December 1907
Withdrawn:	No 2600 – October 1944
	No 2597 – December 1946
	No 2601 – January 1948
	Nos 32001/3 – July 1948
	No 32004 – November 1948
	Nos 32006/7/10/598/9/604 –
	September 1948
	Nos 32009/603 – April 1951
	Nos 32005/8/595/6/602 – June 1951
	No 32002 – July 1951

*Note: The weight differences between the batches, with the second series of engines gaining half a ton over their lives by comparison with the later series seems to be attributable simply to different ways of weighing engines or from the substitution of the inherited cast-iron wheel centres of the later series being replaced by cast-steel ones later in their lives.

Class I2
10 locomotives in class

Numbers:
11-20 (LBSCR)
B11-20 (SR to 1931)
2011-20 (SR from 1931)

Weight in working order:	68 tons 10 cwt
Boiler pressure:	170lb sq inch
Cylinders:	17½in x 26in
Tractive effort:	17,430 lb
Driving-wheel diameter:	5ft 6in
Valve gear:	Stephensons, slide valves
Delivered:	No 11 – December 1907

No 12 – March 1908
Nos 13/14 – April 1908
No 15 – May 1908
No 16 – June 1908
Nos 17-19 – July 1908
No 20 – August 1908

Nos 80/1 – December 1910
Nos 82-5 – June 1912
No 86 – September 1912
Nos 87/8 – November 1912
No 89 – December 1912
Nos 90/1 – March 1913

Withdrawn:	No 2011 – January 1933
	No 2014 – February 1933
	No 2016 – September 1933
	No 2012 – March 1933
	No 2015 – January 1936
	No 2020 – February 1936
	No 2018 – April 1936
	No 2019* – November 1937
	No 2017* – January 1938
	No 2013 – January 1939

*Note: 2013/19 were sold to the War Department for further use on the Longmoor Military Railway.

Class I3
27 locomotives in class

Numbers:
21-30/75-91(LBSCR)
B21-30/75-91 (SR to 1931)
2021-30/75-91 (SR from 1931)
32021-23/25-30/75-91 (BR)

Weight in working order (as built):	No 21 – 73 tons 0 cwt
	No 22 – 74 tons 0 cwt
	Nos 27-30/75/6 74 tons 10 cwt
	Nos 23-6/77-91 76 tons 0 cwt
Boiler pressure:	No 21 – 180lb sq in
	No 22 – 140 (later 160)lb sq in
	Nos 23-30/75-91 160 (later 180)lb sq in
Cylinders:	Nos 21/27-30/75/6 – 19in x 26in
	Nos 22-26/77-91 – 21in x 26in
Tractive effort:	22,065lb
Driving-wheel diameter:	6ft 9in
Valve gear:	No 21 – Stephensons, slide valves
	Nos 22-30/75-91 – Stephensons, piston valves
Delivered:	No 21 – December 1907
	No 22 – March 1908
	No 23 – February 1909
	Nos 24-6 – March 1909
	No 27 – May 1909
	Nos 28/9 – December 1909
	Nos 30/75/6 – March 1910
	No 77 – October 1910
	Nos 78/9 – November 1910

Withdrawn:	No 2024 – November 1944
	No 32025 – January 1950
	No 32080 – March 1950
	No 32085 – July 1950
	Nos 32087/8 – October 1950
	Nos 32079/90 – November 1950
	No 32076 – December 1950
	No 32078 – January 1951
	Nos 32027/9 – February 1951
	Nos 32077/84 – March 1951
	No 32089 – April 1951
	No 32022 – May 1951
	Nos 32082/3 – June 1951
	No 32023 – July 1951
	Nos 32026/30/81 – August 1951
	Nos 32021/8 – September 1951
	Nos 32075/86 – October 1951
	No 32091 – May 1952

Note that the prototype, No 32021, was amongst the last to go whilst the last built, No 32091, was the last survivor.

Class H2
6 locomotives in class

Numbers:
421-6 (LBSCR)
B421-6 (SR to 1931)
2421-6 (SR from 1931)
32421-6 (BR, 32423 not carried)

Weight in working order:	69 tons 15 cwt (engine)
Boiler pressure:	170 (later 200)lb sq in
Cylinders:	21in x 26in
Tractive effort:	20,840lb
Driving-wheel diameter:	6ft 7½in
Valve gear:	Stephensons, piston valves
Delivered:	No 421 – June 1911
	No 422 – July 1911
	Nos 423/4 – September 1911
	No 425 – December 1911
	No 426 – January 1912
Withdrawn:	No 2423 – May 1949
	Nos 32421/6 – August 1956
	Nos 32422/5 – September 1956
	No 32424 – April 1958

II: Names

Despite the fact that in William Stroudley's time all Brighton locomotives bore names (a policy perpetuated by his successor, Robert Billinton), none of the Brighton Atlantics was initially named, Douglas Earle Marsh considering the practice obsolete. However, Lawson Billinton reintroduced the naming of selected locomotives following the Brighton Board's requirement to name Marsh's solitary Class J1 Pacific *Abergavenny* to honour the Stroudley locomotive whose number it had taken. This policy was not implemented retrospectively, but when on 14 June 1913 the French President, M Raymond Poincaré, made an official state visit to the United Kingdom, 'H1' Atlantic No 39 was specially prepared to work the Royal Train from Portsmouth Harbour to London Victoria, being named *La France* for the occasion. It retained the name until the remainder of the 'H1s' and 'H2s' were named by the Southern Railway in the mid-1920s, becoming *Hartland Point* in January 1926. Details of the namings are as follows:

Loco number	Date named	Name	Location of geographical landmark
37	March 1926	*Selsey Bill*	South of Chichester, West Sussex
38	May 1925	*Portland Bill*	Portland, Weymouth, Dorset
39	June 1913	*La France*	On the other side of La Manche!
39	January 1926	*Hartland Point*	North Devon coast west of Bideford
40	July 1925	*St. Catherine's Point*	Southernmost tip of the Isle of Wight
41	March 1925	*Peveril Point*	Swanage, Dorset
421	February 1926	*South Foreland*	Dover, Kent
422	June 1925	*North Foreland*	Broadstairs, Kent
423	April 1927	*The Needles*	Westernmost tip of the Isle of Wight
424	June 1926	*Beachy Head*	Eastbourne, East Sussex
425	August 1926	*Trevose Head*	Padstow, Cornwall
426	June 1925	*St. Alban's Head*	Swanage, Dorset

The names chosen were those of substantial headlands in Southern Railway territory, although it is worth noting that St Alban's Head is more correctly known as St Aldhelm's Head.

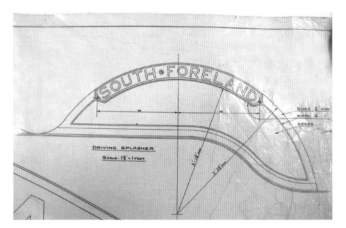

ABOVE AND RIGHT These photographs show the original Southern Railway drawings for the nameplates used on the 'H1' and 'H2' Atlantics.

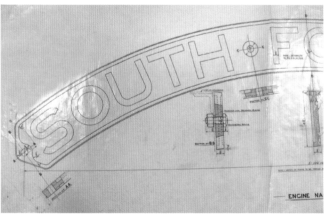

The two 'Saints' had their sainthood denoted by the abbreviation 'ST', both letters being capitals (and the same size as all other letters) with a full stop after the T.

The drawings are in the care of the National Railway Museum at York.

ABOVE The nameplates produced by the Southern Railway for the Atlantic tender engines followed the Company's standard form as adopted for use on the 'Lord Nelson' and Schools' class engines. The 'plates themselves were artfully curved to match the contour of the rear driving wheel splashers and used the standard letter font.

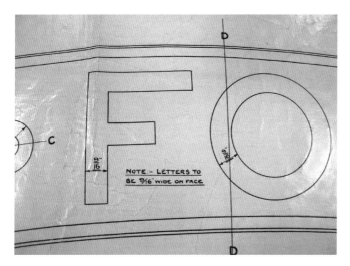

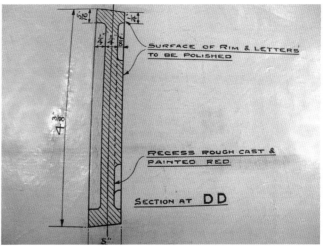

III: The 'Leader' project

The following excerpt from Kevin Robertson's book *The Leader Project – Fiasco or Triumph?* (Ian Allan Publishing, 2007 and 2009) provides a fascinating insight into this abortive line of Southern locomotive development and its relevance to the Brighton Atlantic story.

Generations of railway enthusiasts visiting railway workshops – and even preserved railways today – have gleefully recorded the numbers of the machines they have seen, either complete or otherwise. Indeed, I recall reading with some wry amusement controversy relating to 'when a cop is a cop' – if the number of the engine is visible but there are perhaps no frames or wheels, does it still count? Or if the cab is in a heap on its own, does that count? It's a question of personal preference, but today, when preserved engines swap identities for little more than clever marketing, difficulties can arise – even more so when the stampings of other long-scrapped machines are found on common parts such as rods, wheels and axles. How much of a preserved engine is indeed original and how much is a 'new' replacement?

Why bring this up? Well, work on 'Leader' was approved to commence on 5 September 1946, although it was actually almost a year later in July 1947 that physical construction started. Therefore anyone visiting Brighton Works after the latter date and for the almost two years that it took to complete the engine could well claim to have 'spotted' it in its varying stages of completion.

Why Brighton was chosen is of interest, as it was then the only one of the three Southern Railway workshops (the others being Ashford and Eastleigh) that was considered to have spare capacity, allied to which it was also the location of the head office of the Chief Mechanical Engineer's department. Even so, most of the components were manufactured or machined at Eastleigh – the boiler, wheels, sleeves, etc. On 19 February 1949 an RCTS visit to Eastleigh reported that components for the 'Leader' class – wheels, boilers and other parts – were on view. In effect Brighton acted as an assembly plant in addition to being involved in the fabrication of the numerous items made from sheet. Whether Ashford, or indeed any other outside builder, was charged with the provision of any components is not recorded.

While the 'Leader' and her sisters were in the initial stages of construction, elsewhere on the Southern Railway other experimentation was taking place regarding ideas that Bulleid anticipated would be incorporated in the main design. Timescale-wise this was perhaps strange, as the more usual procedure would be to conduct, then analyse the results and data from, any experimentation prior to inclusion. With the 'Leader' project this was not done. As already mentioned, the new Labour Government had been in power since late July 1945, with the avowed intent of future nationalisation of a number of former privately owned industries including the railways. Although the House of Commons did not actually approve railway nationalisation until December 1946, there can be no doubt that this policy had been promoted as part of the original election manifesto and consequently there would have been both awareness and discussion of the topic in the boardroom of the

Southern before this time. Consequently Bulleid would have known that his timescale was limited.

Experimentation thus first took place involving 'U1' 2-6-0 No 1896 following its overhaul at Ashford in mid-1946. The experiment was not immediately visible to the naked eye, however, as it involved the provision of an opening duct at the base of the smokebox, which was operated mechanically from the cab. Its purpose was to provide an opportunity to dispose of smokebox ashes, char and cinders at intervals during the journey, thus avoiding the otherwise necessary task of cleaning the smokebox at the journey's end. (This was similar to F. W. Webb's experiments on the LNWR in 1870.)

In theory this was a valiant scheme. The duct was only intended to be open on occasions and was thus unlikely to impair steaming in what should otherwise be a sealed environment. In practice, however, it is not believed that any truly useful data was obtained, simply because No 1896 was fresh from overhaul and therefore unlikely to reveal ideal results. A similar remotely controlled duct was later fitted to No 36001 for a time, but drivers soon became aware that its operation would result in particles of ash settling around the edge of the opening, preventing an airtight seal being formed. (It is rumoured that a supply of dung was carried, which, when surreptitiously applied to the edges, produced the desired effect. No comment was made concerning the additional aroma that may have resulted …) It is believed that No 1896 ran in this condition for only a short time, and no formal trial results have been discovered.

The matter of ash cleaning on the 'Leader' was perhaps the first of numerous aspects of the design that were clearly given little thought when the decision was eventually taken to settle for coal firing. The enclosed environment of the smokebox and cab made ash disposal difficult, to say the least. The duct as fitted would have been of little practical use, save for depositing grit on to the moving parts – again perhaps contributory to later bogie problems.

A second, far more serious form of experimentation commenced in July 1947, when former LBSCR 'H1'- class 4-4-2 No 2039 *Hartland Point* was withdrawn from capital service to be fitted with sleeve valves, which were then being proposed for the 'Leader' design. Here again the question is 'Why?' With this experiment in mind, it would seem that a final decision had already been made that the 'Leader' would be so equipped. If so, why bother with the experiments if the decision was already a fait accompli?

Brighton stripped No 2039 of its original outside cylinders and front bogie, and in their place new cylinders were installed, fabricated from a steel shell with exhaust annuli at either end and single central admission annuli. Within the cylinder was a cast-iron liner made of fine-grade 'Mechanite'. Within this liner, and sealed with no fewer than 30 rings, was another Mechanite-grade sleeve valve, around the circumference of which were machined openings to correspond with the admission and exhaust openings of the liner. Finally, within the sleeve came the piston, although as would be expected the original bore was thus considerably reduced: the original 26in stroke was unaltered, but the 19in diameter became only 14 inches. Tractive effort measured at the standard 85% of boiler pressure was thus reduced from 20,070lb to 11,892lb, which in theory meant that the boiler would always have plenty in reserve, although the pulling-power of the engine would be considerably reduced.

It has been suggested that both these and the later similar sleeves for the 'Leader' were machined on an old lathe at Eastleigh, which had originated from the former LSWR works at Nine Elms, being the only one on the Southern that could accommodate the size of the item to be machined. Operated by just one man, it took up almost the length of one wall within the Eastleigh machine shop. As the sleeves for *Hartland Point* and the 'Leader' were similar in length, it is reasonable to assume that all were produced in the same way.

The bogie alteration was necessary as the original item would foul what were both larger and wider replacement cylinders; it was thus replaced with the wheels from a 'D3' tank, which were of 3ft diameter compared to the original 3ft 6in. (According to *The Railway Observer* the wheels used originated from 'D3' No 2366. This particular engine was not officially withdrawn until February 1949, but it could of course have been standing around out of use for some time. Another possibility is that the bogie came from No 2363, which was withdrawn in December 1947. There is also some doubt as to whether just the wheelsets were changed, or if an actual 'D3' front bogie was fitted.)

In addition to the cylinder changes, a multiple-jet blastpipe was fitted, and a new chimney. The location of the Westinghouse air pump was also altered to the right-hand side of the framing from its original position on the left.

Operation of the valves was cleverly thought out, for in addition to a fore-and-aft motion a degree of axial rotation was imparted to the sleeves. The actual percentage figure has not been accurately determined, but from photographs it would appear to have been something in the order of 25° either side of the horizontal. As such, the valves in operation when viewed from the front imparted a 'figure of eight' motion while at the same time sliding back and forth.

The fore-and-aft motion was achieved by extending the ordinary valve spindles attached to the Stephenson link motion allied to rocking levers ahead of the frames, and protruding to either side. This was in some ways visually similar to the method used for controlling the valves of the outside cylinders on Great Western four-cylinder types. The axial rotation worked via a rotating shaft beneath the smokebox, which was itself driven through a Morse inverted tooth chain off the leading coupled axle. Two new mechanical lubricators were also driven by this rotating shaft.

The axial rotation was provided in an attempt to equalise both wear and temperature, both of which could otherwise cause fracture. Another possible cause of fracture would be lack of lubrication, so numerous oil feeds were fitted, all pump-driven from two Wakefield mechanical lubricators mounted in a far from ideal place at the base of the smokebox. No 2039 was not fitted with an opening ash duct.

Work on No 2039 progressed through the summer and autumn of 1947, with the engine finally ready for a steam test within the workshops on 5 November. At this stage no rings had been fitted, so understandably the results were clouded, in more than one sense. A further external trial was arranged for 3 December, with Bulleid present; also invited was his brother-in-law, H. G. Ivatt, who held the CME's position on the LMS. No 2039 ran up and down the Brighton

Works yard, but was still devoid of sealing rings, so the front was still shrouded in escaping steam.

Two weeks then elapsed, during which the 60 sealing rings were fitted, and No 2039 was steamed again on 15 December ready for its first run, albeit light-engine. This was made as far as Lewes in company with 'E5' No 2404, the operating authorities seemingly determined to ensure there would be no breakdowns and consequent disruption of traffic. Without the benefit of any formal report, it is difficult to be exact about the results, although it is known that a number of rings broke on this first run and were replaced at Brighton Works.

Bulleid's aim in using sleeve valves was to increase the efficiency of the steam usage by reducing losses caused by condensation. The sleeve valve allowed virtually the whole cylinder to be permanently enveloped in a steam jacket, which became in effect a circular steam chest. This 'steam chest' afforded a volume some 3¼ times the cylinder capacity at maximum cut-off, 75%. With the addition of the large steam inlet and exhaust annuli, a free flow for the steam was ensured, with consequential free running.

However, any advantage gained was offset by the increases in mechanical complexity and identified difficulties due to friction losses. It would take the various test runs to establish if a steam-tight seal could indeed be maintained, especially across the exhaust ports and front radial outlet slots for the extension drive lugs.

No 2039 on test

The seasonal traffic peak of Christmas 1947 no doubt precluded any serious attempt at test running with No 2039 until the start of 1948, so it was not until the first day of public ownership, 1 January, that No 2039 worked former SECR three-coach set No 597 between Brighton and Eastbourne. (It is believed that this same three-coach set was used on a number of occasions behind No 2039.) This was an empty stock working, the guard instructed to ensure that passengers were not permitted to join the train at the various station stops that were made in order to provide information as to the acceleration characteristics of the engine in its modified form.

At this stage all was well, and no doubt buoyed by the success there followed what was an almost daily test, again northeast from Brighton, to Groombridge via Lewes, a distance of some 30 miles. Although not stated as such, it is reasonable to assume that the train was able to use the nearby triangle to turn, and return the same way. Again it is unfortunate that no formal records of these trials have survived, although the runs would undoubtedly have been monitored by members of the Brighton test section. What is known is that the modifications appeared to bear out the hope for a free-running engine, with 70-80mph reached with ease.

Some time in the same month there were also some light-engine trials to Three Bridges in company with a 'K'-class Mogul, which was evidently propelled by No 2039 in both directions. The presence of the extra engine was again no doubt a means of insurance against breakdown on what was the main London line.

Enough confidence had by now presumably been gained to find No 2039 a more cost-effective role, so from February 1948 she was put to work on trains of carriage underframes between Lancing and

Eastleigh. Whether these were one-way trips with the engine returning light from Hampshire is not certain.

Unfortunately, however, by now all was not well, for despite the limited mileage actually covered, No 2039 had developed a capacity for prolific consumption of water, and no doubt coal, so the fireman's work would have been similarly increased. Rumour has it that No 2039 would leave Brighton for Lancing and Eastleigh with a full tender tank, but would have to stop for water at least twice en route. Usually these stops were at Chichester and Fareham, and this on a run totalling no more than some 65 miles. This equated to something in the order of between 53 and 87 gallons per mile, up to 3½ times what would usually have been expected. To evaporate this amount of water the equivalent coal consumption was also high, and likely to have been in the order of 60lb per mile. Not unexpectedly, therefore, the engine was observed back in the works by the end of the same month, February 1948.

Repairs – or modifications – were undoubtedly carried out, and between March and June there were a number of runs from Brighton to either Lewes or, it is stated, Cowden, just north of Groombridge. There was at least one run to Hastings, as evidenced by the accompanying timings sheet for Saturday 29 May 1948 (which relates just to the anticipated timings to be achieved and does not mean that the trial either took place or was indeed completed).

It is not known if the other runs were all light-engine or with empty stock in tow, although certain of the Cowden trips involved a single bogie utility van and two Royal Mail vans, Nos 4951/2. The latter two vehicles are reported as specially allocated to this working.

What is certain is that in June a three-coach set was taken from Brighton to Tunbridge Wells West at least once, after which the same load was worked on several occasions between Brighton and Hastings – possibly to the latter location at similar timings to those mentioned above. As at the start of 1948, the results were again encouraging, so the load was increased to between four and five bogie vehicles once more to Tunbridge Wells West, a working that continued twice daily until some time in July.

The rest of July and August 1948 are something of a mystery, but it is known that in September 1948 No 2039 was seen at the head of a train of bogie utility vans, although the destination and whether it was empty stock is not certain.

Details for the autumn of 1948 are likewise uncertain, but No 2039 is known to have been in Brighton Works again for much of this time. Possibly little actual progress in the way of maintenance or repairs/modifications was actually made, and the length of time out of service could well be because any previous urgency had already 'evaporated', and Brighton was running at almost full capacity with its Light Pacific building programme, as well as the construction of No 36001 and the other normal repair projects.

December 1948 also did not seem to bother the operating department as much as the previous year in so far as using No 2039 was concerned, for at the start of the month there were a series of light-engine runs as far as Hastings, often twice each day and usually at weekends. Then on 19 December came the chance to excel, for the engine was set the task of hauling an Officers' Special between Ashford and Brighton (how the engine came to be at Ashford is not

reported). All was well until the train left St Leonards, near Hastings, when there was a sudden fracture of the right-hand valve rod. Who was on the train and the purpose of the special is not reported, but it cannot have done the credibility of No 2039 any good, as the motion had to be completely taken down in the nearby shed yard, followed by a tow back to Brighton.

For almost three months nothing is known, although it may be reasonable to assume that No 2039 simply languished at Brighton. However, during this time it was also obviously repaired, for on 14 March 1949 it is reported to have been in charge of a revenue-earning passenger service, the three coaches of the Hastings–Birkenhead through service, which No 2039 was booked to work between Brighton and Redhill. In view of her previous unpredictable performance and the fact this was a main-line working, it was perhaps surprising that no pilot was provided; presumably someone behind the scenes had exerted pressure to ensure that a sleeve-valve engine could be entrusted to work in a reliable fashion. It does not take a genius to imagine who that authority probably was, although the faith was rewarded, for both the outward and return workings were accomplished without difficulty. This would be the only time that No 2039 would ever work a fare-paying passenger service. (The Birkenhead through trains had only been reinstated a few months earlier on 27 September 1948 after a lapse of some nine years. SR/GWR stock was used on alternate days, with No 2039's task classified as Brighton Duty No 530. At Redhill the Hastings portion was attached to one from Margate and Dover and the service then continued towards Reading and its ultimate destination.)

Two days later the engine worked an empty three-coach set north from Brighton to Redhill again, and, as on 14 March, without a pilot. All was well until Earlswood, when adverse signals were encountered – due, it is believed, to the train running early, evidencing the free-running characteristics of No 2039 once again. Unfortunately, however, when a 'clear' indication was received No 2039 stubbornly refused to move in either direction. Later examination revealed that the engine had stopped with the ports in a totally 'blind' position, which meant that no steam could enter the cylinders regardless of the setting of the reversing gear. Whether this was a fault in design, manufacture, assembly or valve setting was never revealed (perhaps never even investigated and established!).

Delays to other traffic were mounting, so 'E' class 4-4-0 No 31587 was hastily summoned to drag No 2039 and her train the final short distance to Redhill, other services being delayed by almost 25 minutes. The return to Brighton later in the day was made with the same pilot engine – clearly this time no chances were being taken.

Some form of alteration was no doubt carried out, as on 1 April – the date would have a somewhat wry irony later – No 2039 again ventured out, this time on a three-coach special from Brighton to Ashford and routed via the coast line and Hastings. Bulleid and another member of his senior staff were on the footplate as observers and were thus able to view at first hand the difficulties experienced by the driver in restarting after a signal stop near Ore. The record reveals that some 7½ minutes were spent in attempting this restart.

The final confirmed run in which No 2039 participated (although no date is given) took place a short time later when the engine was again rostered to head what was deemed a 'works train' between Lancing and Eastleigh, thought to have consisted of four passenger vehicles.

After this came a period of open store at Brighton until the engine entered the works on 14 June 1949 with the somewhat strange intention of restoring it to its original form; however, as referred to earlier, the class was already considered life-expired, so instead No 2039 remained untouched inside the works pending a decision regarding her future.

Somewhat surprisingly, that decision was for overhaul but with the sleeve valves retained, so No 2039 was given what would in effect be a major refurbishment, which even included a replacement boiler sent especially from Eastleigh. She emerged by 2 September 1949 as BR No 32039 painted in unlined black, but perhaps significantly without any ownership insignia or wording. Presumably some test running would have been involved following the overhaul, but this is not reported.

Following overhaul – and presumably a satisfactory period of trial (and running-in?) – the engine was allocated to Brighton shed and intended for normal work. How this could seriously have been anticipated must be open to question, as unless some major

modifications had been made she would surely have behaved in exactly the same way as before. Indeed, her reputation was known and, possibly due to instructions from the shed management, she was always ignored and may never have been used as intended.

The rest of 1949, all of 1950, and the start of 1951 were spent in the same way, the engine obviously deteriorating in store without being used. In February 1951 official notice was received to move No 32039 to Eastleigh for assessment, but inspection at Brighton revealed that she was unsuitable to make the journey under her own power (whether this was a boiler defect is not reported), and she was instead towed to Hampshire by 'C2X' No 32438.

Not surprisingly, inspection at Eastleigh revealed the same as had been found at Brighton, and that a further overhaul would be required in order to restore the engine to traffic. This time it was not forthcoming, and No 32039 quietly disappeared from the scene, being noted on the scrap lines at the works on 24 February 1951. She was finally dismantled at Eastleigh in March 1951, although at least one of the nameplates survived.

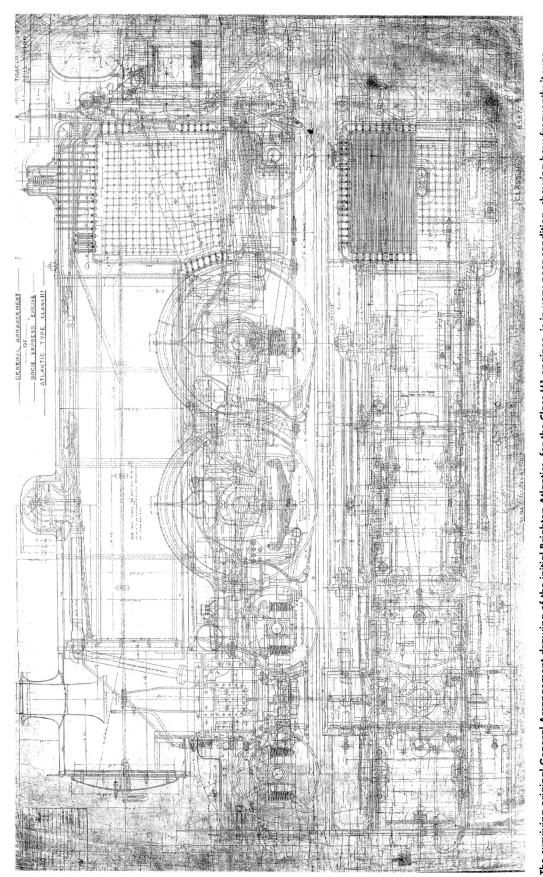

GENERAL ARRANGEMENT
OF
BOGIE EXPRESS ENGINE
ATLANTIC TYPE CLASS H1

The surviving original General Arrangement drawing of the initial Brighton Atlantics, for the Class H1 engines, is in very poor condition, showing how frequently it was amended and referred to by the various engineering staff during the lifetime of this class. It is included here as it is historically important in the history of the Brighton Atlantics, but it should be noted that it is not a Great Northern Railway drawing with red-ink alterations! National Railway Museum

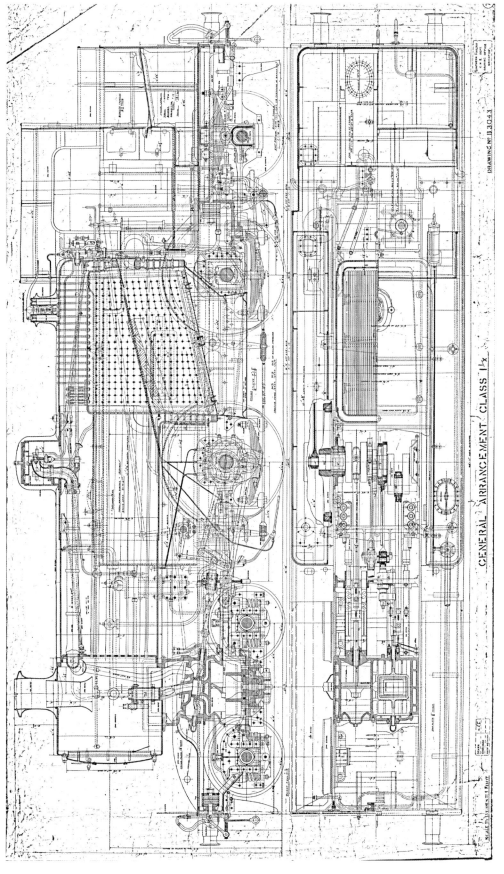

The General Arrangement drawing of the rebuilt Class 11X, the rather more successful version of the original Marsh Atlantic tanks. *National Railway Museum*

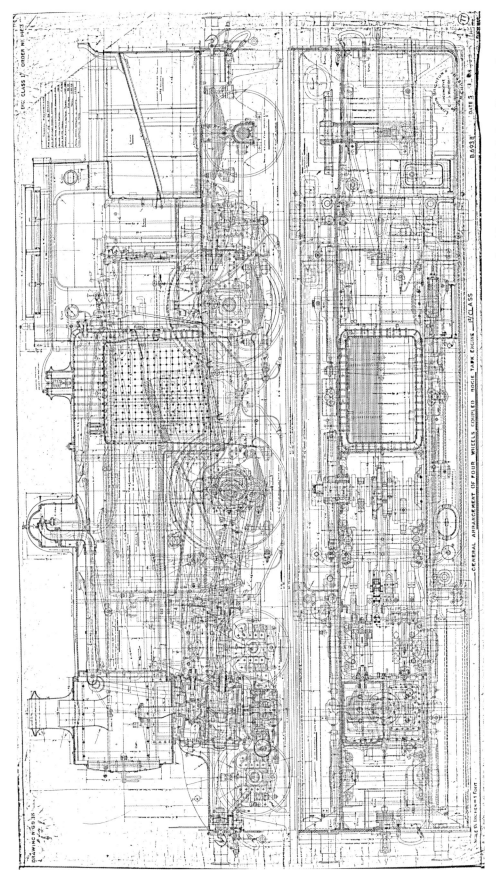

Like the G/A drawing for the 'H1' Atlantic, the drawing held by the National Railway Museum for the '12' class shows considerable use but is included to allow readers to compare the '12' with its later development, the '14' class. National Railway Museum

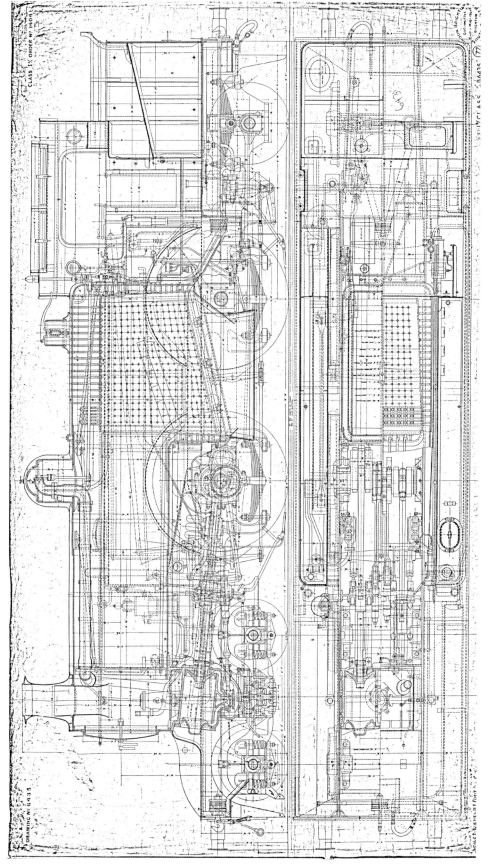

THIS PAGE AND OVERLEAF G/As for the two principal varieties of Class 13 locomotives, Saturated with Slide Valves and Superheated with Piston Valves.

National Railway Museum

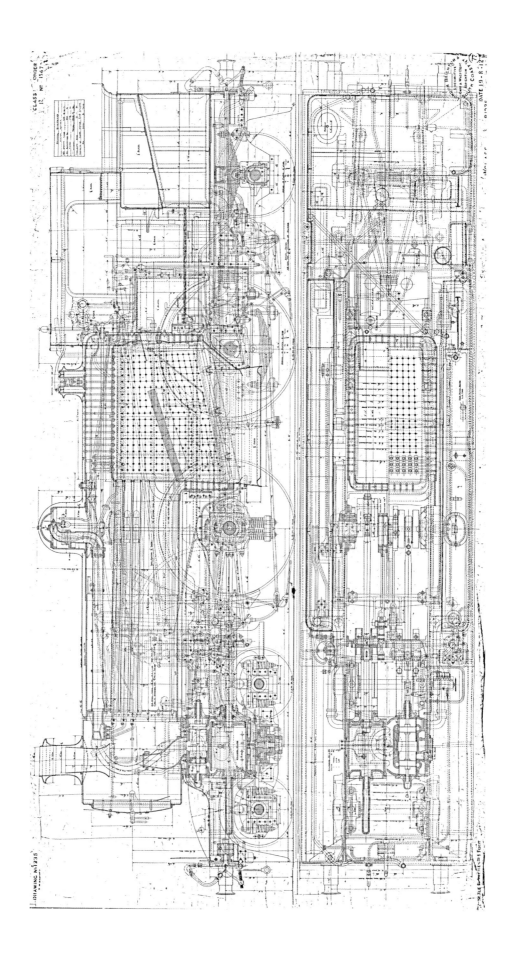

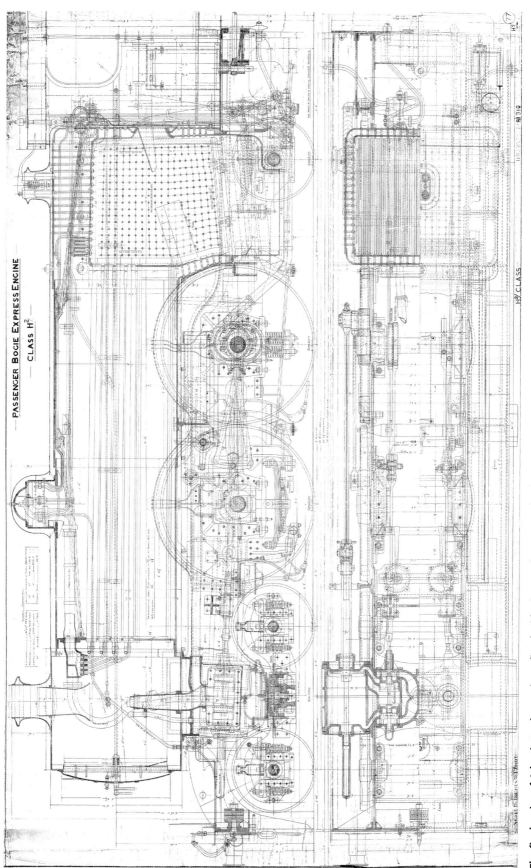

PASSENGER BOGIE EXPRESS ENGINE

CLASS H²

The final series of Atlantic tender engines, fitted with piston valves. National Railway Museum

INDEX